HM

JUST AROUND THE CORNER

JUST AROUND THE CORNER

by

HUMPHREY PHELPS

Illustrations by Hugh Moss

Published in 1974

by

The Thornhill Press
7 Russell Street
Gloucester

ISBN 0 9501544 9 0

Printed by Stoate & Blackwell Ltd. 15/16 Bennington Street, Cheltenham.

Life is a jest, and all things show it;
I thought so once, but now I know it.

John Gay.

For my own boys

CONTENTS

Our story opens on a Saturday afternoon in early 1938. A small boy and his mother are walking along the High Street of a village somewhere in West Gloucestershire.

Chapter 1

UNCLE GEORGE

AS Mother and I came round the corner, we saw Uncle George leaning against the Post Office wall, his head buried in an arm. He was making a terrible noise. Knowing how he was always besieged with ailments I immediately thought that he'd been overcome by some sort of attack. "Whoo! whoo! whoo!" he howled. Poor Uncle George, perhaps this was the beginning of the end of him, perhaps he'd been overtaken by some terrible affliction which not even his large collection of remedies could counteract.

We quickened our pace and Mother's face lengthened as her eyes widened like saucers. In a woebegone voice, and Mother was excellent at woebegone voices, she said, "He's gone off his head at last, I knew it was only a matter of time. It's to be hoped he doesn't hang on long, that's all, when they're like that the sooner they go the better — you run along and get Dr. Higgins, and on the way back get the policeman. He may be obstreperous and if I know anything about George he'll give the maximum amount of trouble and fuss. Always did when he was in his right mind, so there's every reason to think he'll be worse now."

We were within four or five yards of him before it became apparent that he was convulsed with laughter, "Whoo! whoo! whoo!"

He was too busy laughing to notice us. A couple of Mother's friends passed by on the other side of the street pretending not to notice us, but when they were safely past they turned round and had a good look. Then they walked on, heads together, obviously having the matter over.

For a moment Mother just stood there studying Uncle George's quivering form in disgust. Then, when her friends were out of earshot, she spoke. "George," she said sharply, "whatever's the matter with you?"

His laughter slowed until it became a sort of gurgle. He slowly turned to face us. "Ooh, ooh, ooh, nothing's the matter with me, never felt better in me life bar a touch of wind, I'm absolutely first class." He became serious and said confidentially, "Those powders that I read about on Sunday, just on the market, are Al. I bought half-a-dozen packets in town on Tuesday and they've worked wonders, cleared up my trouble in no time at all. You ought to get some, Ethel, p'raps they'd do you a bit of good."

"I don't want any of your quacky trish-trash, or any catchpenny rubbish. What I do want to know is why you were making that disgusting noise if there's nothing the matter with you?"

"Whoo! whoo! whoo! I just thought of something funny and stopped to have a good laugh about it."

"Well, I wish you'd find somewhere more private to do it, making such an exhibition of yourself in a public place." Mother suddenly started sniffing in a very ostentatious way. "George," she said disapprovingly, "I believe you're the worse for drink."

"Daz and set it, Ethel, I'm always the better for drink."

"You're a downright disgrace to us all, George. After this degrading conduct I shall never be able to hold my head up at W.I. meetings. Mrs. Peabody and Mrs. Gosworth both saw your terrible behaviour."

"You ask Mrs. Peabody what she was doing in the spinney last Thursday night; that'll shut her up, Ethel, that'll soon make her laugh the other side of her face, I'll warrant."

"Good day to you, George," said Mother, and to me she said tersely, "C'mon." I looked back over my shoulder and Uncle George gave me a large slow wink.

"Oh that man," said Mother, as we made our way home. "Oh that disgusting man, that horrible old man, he'll be the death of me and — and he'll be the ruination of you. Your Father ought to speak to him, but he's soft when it comes to that George. Your Father's putty in that man's hands and so are you. You'll never lift a finger to help me. When did you last chop any sticks for me? You'd let me heave my inside out mowing the lawn, while you sit guzzling cider down at that cratur's. You never put a spade in our garden, but you'll dig, dig for him."

"But Mother, I've helped you to-day," I said.

"Yes, but only because you couldn't find him at home. I can tell you where he was, in that wretched Lion drinking himself silly. I'm tormented by all of you and if I have much more of it I think I shall go clean out of my mind. I'm sure he does it on purpose to annoy me, he knows I never liked him. He's a nasty morbid thing — murder, scandal, illness and drink, that's all that man thinks about, that, and filling that great stomach of his. And all those patent medicines — his stomach must be like a chemist's shop — no wonder it bulges. I'd like to ram the lot down his fat throat at once, and that rancid bacon of his."

"Oh Mother, he's very good to us — look at the pigmeat and liver and stuff he gave you when he killed his pig a few weeks ago."

"Huh", snorted Mother, "a sprat to catch a mackerel! Dumped that on me with a great show of generosity — and after all I do for him too — and then the cratur asked me to make his faggots." Mother was now in full spate. "Then look what happened last night, dragged your father off to that wretched Lion and kept him out all hours of the night — never mind me, I could sit there and rot for all that they cared — and when your father does finally come home he's silly and glassy-eyed and says 'Our George was in fine form tonight'. I soon told him I couldn't stand that George in any shape or form whatsoever."

Mother regarded Uncle George as a threat to respectability and a bad influence on everybody; also, I suspect, she was jealous of the affection Father and I had for him. She couldn't see that in Uncle George's company life became richer, livelier and more comical. In Uncle George's presence the most extraordinary things could and did happen. It is true he was gloomy and solemn at times or at least

11

pretended to be, but not for long; a kind of effervescence within him soon turned everything to merriment. He had his setbacks, many of his schemes went awry, but his natural buoyancy soon had him on top again.

Uncle George visited the doctor at least once a week. Sometimes he would go into the surgery to see Dr. Higgins and would come out with a bottle of red medicine. Some people said that Dr. Higgins had a five gallon cask labelled 'George's Mixture', but I don't think that was true. Usually he just dropped into the waiting room for a chat; he asked the waiting patients about their ailments and gave them advice and then, like at the White Lion and the Post Office, he gossiped. "Mind," he'd say, rubbing a finger on the side of his nose and furrowing his brow, "don't let on I told you, but," and now he'd puff his cheeks, "it's a true bill."

At home he'd discuss the murders and scandals he'd read about in the *News of the World*. Father would listen wide-eyed and shocked or perhaps hang his head in his hands and every few minutes mutter, "There's some devilish bad baggers about, George." All the newspapers, for weeks on end, were full of a murder not more than twenty miles away from where we lived. The Haw Bridge Mystery or the Torso Murder it was called. Though the police dragged the river and scoured the surrounding countryside, the head was never found and the mystery was never solved. Sunday after Sunday Uncle George and Father discussed the gory details and formulated theories. Uncle reeled off a list of detectives, barristers and pathologists as if they were personal friends. Spilsbury, Birkett and others had, one would almost think, consulted Uncle George about some difficult problem at some time or other.

They'd sit in the living-room, one on either side of the fireplace, completely engrossed in their talk and oblivious of Mother's presence. She would get a duster and aggressively flip it, or push the carpet sweeper round them, but the only time they noticed her was when Father wanted a cup of tea. "Oh Ethel", he'd say, "we're as dry as bones, make us a cup of tea and bring our George a few nice biscuits, he's bound to be feeling peckish."

Mother would flounce out of the room, muttering, "I've got to wait on you hand, foot and finger and what thanks do I get." Nevertheless she'd make the tea because however much she might mutter, complain, and threaten, she always obeyed Father.

Chapter 2

THE BAKERY

UNCLE George was Father's brother and considerably older. Unlike Father who was small and wiry, Uncle George was large and stout. His large, round, rubicund face was wrinkled and clean shaven — by clean shaven I mean he had no beard, moustache or mutton chop whiskers, although he often went unshaven, a thick grey stubble of whiskers usually covered his chin. As for the wrinkles, well Mother said they came from pulling dreadful faces. She was right about the dreadful faces; he could pull a seemingly endless variety of grotesque faces, and frequently did so for my amusement, but, as with almost everything else he did, Mother disapproved of these faces and often prophesied that he would stop like it one day and Heaven help the lot of us if he did so, as his normal face was quite enough to put up with.

Although he was in his early fifties, his hair wasn't grey but mousy coloured, he hadn't a lot of hair but what he had was more like wool than hair. It really was most unusual hair. I've never seen anyone else with hair like it, but then I've never met anyone else quite like Uncle George.

He lived alone in a square house, built of stone and roofed with slate, which stood on the outskirts of the village. Long ago, I imagine, it must have served as a farmhouse and it still had a large garden and a couple of orchards attached to it. Uncle George coveted a paddock and another orchard which adjoined and hoped one day to be able to buy them. His main interests, besides those already referred to by Mother, were gardening, fruit growing, pigs and poultry. Uncle George was an expert in these things, even Mother who was critical of all his pursuits, could not gainsay that. Nobody could breed and feed pigs like Uncle, and when it came to gardening he was the district's acknowledged champion. At our local fruit and flower show he swept the deck — the local weekly paper was filled with his name as prizewinner once a year and Uncle always bought half-a-dozen copies of the paper that week.

He also grew roses, sweet peas and chrysanthemums, but no other flowers — he was firmly of the opinion that it was unmanly to grow any other flowers. However, he did have honeysuckle growing over his garden shed and other outhouses, over fences and up old tree stumps. Presumably honeysuckle did not count and neither did the odd clumps of Christmas and Lenten roses, Welsh poppies, lilies of the valley, daffodils and paeonies, because, as he said, "I don't grow 'em, they grow and look after themselves."

Uncle George was a baker by trade and his bakery was in the middle of the village. The shop was small and rather dark and, outside, drab brown paint peeled from window and door. Behind the shop lay the bakehouse, where crickets and cockroaches lived; the warehouse, with its bags of flour; and the office, a poky, dingy place with dust covered ledgers, and receipts stuck on spikes; accounts and other papers littered the high topped desk. Uncle George gave scant attention to his paperwork. Some people, the ones he knew were 'all right', hadn't received a bread bill for years.

Adjoining the bakehouse was the yard where firewood was stacked. In the summer, birds nested in the stacks and sometimes rats would take up residence amongst the firewood too, and then Uncle George would send for Reuben Kimmins, the jobbing builder and also poacher, who kept terrier dogs and ferrets. The three of us would

14

spend a noisy afternoon, "routing out they rats, the varmints", as Uncle put it. Much to the annoyance of Mrs. Peabody, church organist, this routing was almost invariably done on a Sunday afternoon. Reuben, especially after a few pints of beer (and he always spent mid-day Sunday in The White Lion), was none too careful about his language. Mrs. Peabody would rap on the fence. Mr. Peabody was incapable of rapping by three-o'clock on a Sunday afternoon as he would be drunk and asleep, snoring loudly in the back room. Mrs. Peabody didn't know that we knew about that, neither did she know that we knew about her secret meetings in the spinney, but you can't keep things like that dark in a village. Mrs. Peabody would rap on the fence and shout "Can't you have more respect for the Lord's day?"

"There's a durn great rat run under the fence, Ma'am, must be under yer fit," Uncle George would shout, and Mrs. Peabody would scream and rush into her house. "That's got rid of that old besom," Uncle would comment.

Grandfather was a baker and Uncle followed him into the business, but I don't think Uncle ever had his heart and soul in it. The bakery kept him away, but not so much as you might think, from his pigs, garden and orchards. It was a tie, and then there were the whims, fads and fancies of the customers. He never could understand why people wanted bread every day. "I just can't fathom why they want fresh bread, tis no good to 'em, it only gives 'em the wind." Wind was always a trouble to poor Uncle George and he'd never yet found a remedy to counteract it. I heard Mother saying, "People don't like it. George can stand behind that counter squeaking his boots together, but that doesn't fool anybody, he's a disgusting old man. Neither do people like somebody coming to the door with a week's growth of hair on their dirty fat old face and a filthy spotted handkerchief tied round their neck and stinking of pigs. And more often than not the worse for drink." But Mother had been particularly nasty about poor Uncle George ever since the Mrs. Williams affair. And Father replied, "I won't have you keep carrying on about our George, you've always been nasty gritted about him. Look how good he was when we heard them nasty noises out in the garden late at night."

"And what did he do about it?"

"He came out with me to see what it was."

"Neither of you went right outside, you just poked your heads round the door like a couple of frightened Isaacs and you said 'I don't know what it is, and our George don't know what it is' and you both went fast asleep in front of the fire. We could all have been murdered in our beds."

15

"Now Ethel, you shouldn't be like that about George. He stopped here all night."

"Only because he was too frightened to go home, the great fool."

Mother flung her leg in a backward motion and went into the kitchen.

Much as I loved Uncle George, I have to admit there was a lot in what Mother said. He was often delivering bread at eleven or twelve o'clock at night with his horse and van. 'The midnight baker', people called him, and he was never allowed to. forget that he'd once dumped Mrs. Wiggins' loaves in her copper which was filled ready for next day's wash. Next morning, the lid stood six or seven inches above the copper where the soaking bread had swollen overnight. When I'd been out helping with deliveries, I'd often heard people shout, "Is it bread washing night tonight, George?" and he would wave his fist and shout, "Bury the axe."

These deliveries were very protracted affairs, it wasn't as if it was only bread to be delivered, oh dear no, it wasn't as simple as that, there were customers' pigs to be inspected and advice on pigkeeping to be given. In the summer, gardens had to be inspected too, and Uncle would often go to a great deal of trouble, explaining why the customer's garden was not as productive as it should be. Orchards often had to be looked at all the year round, sometimes he'd stop for an hour or two and show someone how to prune apple trees. During winter evenings there was elderberry wine to be sampled. And gossip, gossip all the year round; he'd stop for an hour or more at some places. It got that it was impossible to make calls at some places more than once a week and in a week there can be a great accumulation of news. Then some people in the outlying districts were cut down to only one delivery every ten or twelve days. They didn't like it, they complained, they said they wanted three deliveries a week. Uncle George told them that was unnecessary and unreasonable and also told them repeatedly, "There is no need for you to carp about deliveries, God Bless You, there's always plenty of bread down at the bakehouse for them as wants it." This didn't satisfy some of them, they said they'd change to another baker, and they did.

But, it was Uncle George's habit of allowing tramps to sleep in the bakehouse, in return for stirring the dough, which finally finished his bakery. He disliked getting up early and walking to the bakehouse and somehow or other he managed to find a succession of old men to do the early morning work for him. When a particularly dirty old fellow was found one morning dead over the dough custom dwindled rapidly and Uncle George decided it was time to sell up and devote more time to his pigs and garden.

16

Chapter 3

THE SHOPKEEPERS

MATTHEW Banstead, the man who bought Uncle's bakery, was a stranger, but it wasn't long before the village discovered he was living with two women in the house he bought just beyond the bakery. Everyone was soon talking about it. The women split into factions, some said the dark fat woman was his legal wife, while others thought the short fair woman was, a third group thought neither was his wife, while a fourth were of the opinion that Banstead was a bigamist.

Mother said that she couldn't fancy any bread from there, while Father remarked that it was a damned bad principled way of going on, and Uncle George said, "The man must be a blasted fool, one woman is enough trouble for any man, and thank God I've had enough sense to remain single." He paused, wrinkled his brow and nose, and added, "But, by gum it was a near go with that Mrs. Williams, she almost nabbed me, but rajah rhubarb, I was too wily for her. Her with her apple pies and dumplings, but I was too old a bird to be caught by a trick like that. By gum, it was a close shave though."

Mother's friends, Mrs. Peabody and Mrs. Gosworth, thought the vicar should do something about it. Mrs. Gerrish at the Post Office thought the police should do something, because she said, "The man's a sex maniac like you read about in the *News of the World* and if something isn't done we'll all be murdered in our beds."

Mrs. Gerrish, like Mother, Mrs. Peabody and several other women, lived in perpetual fear of being murdered in their beds. Uncle George used to say that Mrs. Peabody was more likely to be murdered in the spinney. Whenever Mother heard him make allusions to the spinney and Mrs. Peabody, she would fly into a rage and declare that it was all a cock and bull story, a wicked slander. Uncle would chuckle and reply, "Go up to the spinney and see for yourself, Ethel. Go and see your fine friend a billing and cooing with her fancy chap." Father would nod his head and say, "Sure to be right, Ethel, if our George says so." But Mother would be gone before Father finished speaking.

Reuben Kimmins said, "As there's so many unmarried women about, I reckon old Banstead's a public benefactor and should be given a medal or summat."

Mrs. Hatch proclaimed loudly to everybody that she, Mrs. Hatch, would personally write to the Bishop. Mrs. Hatch was the newsagent. Outside the shop was a notice reading; Ebenezer Hatch, Newsagent, Stationer and Confectioner; but Mr. Ebenezer Hatch was rarely seen, he remained in the background and never served in the shop. What he did, and how he fared with the formidable Mrs. Hatch, remained a matter for conjecture.

Mrs. Hatch was an autocrat, she not only ran the shop but also tried to run the village. Customers were allowed to have the daily paper of their choice, but she judged them by that choice. "I can tell what people are by the newspapers they take," she said. "Now Major Mostyn is a gentleman of the first rank, he has *The Times*." Other people were judged in descending order according to their newspapers. Readers of the *Daily Mail*, like my Father and Uncle George, were considered 'sound', but readers of some other newspapers did not fare so well.

Customers were not allowed so free a choice with magazines, which she always called books. She exercised a rigorous censorship and if she disapproved of a magazine she would not supply it. Uncle George was 'allowed' to have *The Farmer and Stockbreeder* and *The Sexton Blake Weekly*. Often they were not delivered punctually and I would be sent to enquire about them. "It's no good worrying me, young man, if W. H. Smith doesn't send them to me I can't deliver them to your Uncle and if the publishers don't send them to W. H. Smith, then they can't be sent on to me. But I am going into town tomorrow to see W. H. Smith and I'll mention it to W. H. Smith."

Sometimes I'd see the missing paper in the shop and say so. "Well then take it and go and don't you ever dare to give me any of your sauce again, young man."

Mrs. Hatch was often talking of going in to see W. H. Smith, — she said W. H. Smith in an emphatic long drawn out whisper. After her

18

visits to Smith's she'd tell her customers confidentially, "I've been in to town to see W. H. Smith." She made her visits sound tremendously important, certainly something far more important than the mundane business of ordering and paying for papers. But what the precise nature of her business was, or how W. H. Smith fared with her, we never discovered.

Mother took *Woman's Journal* and it was always late arriving at our home. Whenever I was sent to enquire about it Mrs. Hatch always gave the same retort, "You tell your Mother that she's the only one who has *Woman's Journal* and our Isabel hasn't finished reading it yet."

Isabel was her daughter, a tall, pale woman of thirty-three or four. According to Mrs. Hatch she was perpetually on the brink of marriage. "Our Isabel's talking to a fine young man, quiet, well-to-do and very nicely spoken too — there'll be wedding bells ringing soon." Wedding bells did ring, but never for Isabel. Her courtships didn't usually last long, though the last one went on for almost two years and when it ended Mrs. Hatch was loud in her condemnation of Isabel's erstwhile lover. "The wretch, the rogue, the scoundrel. He's done a shameful thing to our Isabel. Our Isabel's given up the best years of her life to him. If it wasn't for the fact that our Isabel's suffered more than enough already I'd have the law on the wretch. I'd drag him through the courts, I'd make an example of him and make his name stink. I'd have every shilling off him."

Mrs. Hatch sold biscuits, chocolates and sweets. Before she could sell any hard boiled sweets she had to ram a poker in and around the big glass jars she kept them in. The rest of her sweets and the biscuits were soft, while the chocolate was often mouldy and smelt of mice, but

nobody complained more than once — not if they were wise. If you didn't buy an occasional bar of chocolate or packet of biscuits she'd mutter, "Them as goes elsewhere for their chocolates and biscuits can go elsewhere for their papers."

It was rumoured that someone had once rashly suggested that it was about time we had another newsagent in the village and Mrs. Hatch, on hearing this, had threatened to do all manner of things. She'd see W. H. Smith — and wouldn't W. H. Smith have something to say about it. She'd see her solicitor — he would have something to say too. She'd see the police, the magistrates, the clerk of the Rural District Council, they would soon put a stop to another newsagent. It was against the law to have two newsagents in a village and she was the legal newsagent. Evil-minded people, she said, were trying to deprive her of her livelihood — she would write to her M.P. She made it sound that she had an M.P. all to herself. Even Ebenezer Hatch emerged briefly from the background to make vague but dire threats. Eventually the rumpus died down and no one ever again suggested having another newsagent in the village.

Between the newsagent and The Rose and Crown was the butcher's shop, proprietor Mr. Alfred Tucker, who was a stocky little man with a toothbrush moustache, piggy eyes and fat cheeks rather like the pieces of steak displayed in his window. On Mondays Mr. Tucker was busy in his slaughter house behind the shop, on Tuesdays he attended the fat stock sales at the local cattle market. He set off for market in a brown bowler hat, gaudy tie and shirt; a long dogtooth check jacket, off-white breeches, fawn stockings, brown boots and kid gloves. He looked and no doubt felt no end of a swell. "Arse and pockets," Uncle George muttered when he saw him bouncing and swaggering up the street.

On Tuesday evenings, according to Uncle George, he would stand with legs astride in the tap-room of The Rose and Crown, a glass of whisky in one hand, a cigar in the other, and relate to the assembled company a chronicle of his market activities that day. He could apparently take no more than two or three steps along the street pavement without people stopping to congratulate him on the quality, tenderness and general excellence of his meat; or farmers stopping him and begging him to call and see their prime fat stock, when, he would tell them, "It'll have to be very choice to suit me, very choice indeed."

When he arrived at the sale ring the auctioneer would beam at him and announce to the other buyers, "Ah here comes Mr. Alfred Tucker, now there's a man who knows quality when he sees it." And that very day he had bought the very best animals in the market, or then again, there had been nothing good enough to tempt him to buy. He had a reputation to keep up, nothing but the very best was good enough for him as all his customers could testify.

For the rest of the week Mr. Tucker stood quietly behind the counter of his immaculate shop, with its big marble slab, scrubbed wooden block and gleaming hooks. He wore a striped apron; and a straw hat which he lifted to all his lady customers. All his boastfulness was gone and now his only wish was to please his esteemed customers.

Opposite The Rose and Crown was Mr. Teakle's boot and shoe shop. Mr. Teakle, like his father and grandfather, had once made boots, but now he only sold and repaired them. Uncle George bought my first pair of hob-nailed boots from Mr. Teakle. Mr. Teakle was a quiet, mild-mannered, slightly-built man in his late sixties. He wore pebble glasses and although you couldn't see his eyes properly you knew they were twinkling – indeed, all of Mr. Teakle twinkled, he was the kindest and merriest of men. Mr. Teakle was a Liberal and Lloyd George was his hero. He was always talking about him and always called him Mr. Lloyd George.

"I remember when Mr. Lloyd George brought in his pension scheme," he told me more than once, "and I went into The White Lion and all the men in there were carrying on about it and what they would do to Mr. Lloyd George. I held up my hand and silenced them and told them in no uncertain terms that Mr. Lloyd George was the greatest man this country had ever had. I told them that his Pension Scheme was the finest thing the country had ever had, and that one day they would realise it and thank God for Mr. Lloyd George and his scheme."

Mr. Teakle told me he remembered the time when a local man dare not say that he was anything but a Conservative or he would be unable to get a job, and that even to-day the fear lingered and many a person was reluctant to declare himself a Liberal or Socialist.

I heard few people apart from Mr. Teakle mention politics. Mrs. Hatch, from time to time, would declare that she knew some who were no better than Bolsheviks – she could tell by the papers they took, but she was mentioning no names, let people find out for themselves what vipers they had in their midst.

Father would occasionally shake his head and say, "All the good old 'uns are a dying and what are we left with – a lot of damned agitators."

The two genteel Misses Ponsonby kept The Tearoom at the Cross. They served morning coffee and afternoon teas, with home made cakes and scones. They also made and sold jams, marmalades, apple and quince jellies and lemon curd. A card in the lace curtained window informed passers by that these commodities would be sent by post to any part of the British Isles.

The walls of their tearoom were covered with rose-patterned wallpaper and adorned with religious texts executed in poker work (their father had been a Baptist Minister). The wooden floor was highly polished and four rush seated chairs were positioned at each table. The tables were covered with check gingham cloths and had little brass handbells on them. In the summer they did quite a trade with visitors but they were, Mother said, ladies in reduced circumstances. They were firmly opposed to drink, gambling, vivisection and blood sports and the only time they emerged from their tearoom was to distribute leaflets or to collect signatures for a petition against such activities.

Almost everyone signed the old ladies' petitions; I've even seen Uncle George signing one calling for the banning of alcohol and Reuben Kimmins signing one for the abolition of blood sports.

They both spoke together, and said the same thing. They liked to hear all the news but were never malicious. Nearly everything they heard surprised them, and in unison they would exclaim, "Well to be sure." Neither of them had ever seen the sea and their dearest wish was to visit Weston-super-Mare, but, they said, "We're always so busy, we just cannot get away, you see."

Both the Misses Ponsonby had a high opinion of Uncle George and always called him, 'Sir'. Uncle George treated them with the utmost courtesy and was on his best behaviour in their presence. He took gooseberries, raspberries, blackcurrants, apples and quinces for them to make into jam or jelly. They would demur when he offered them as a gift; though they must have been poor their pride would not allow them to accept anything without offering to pay. "Now, now, ladies" Uncle George would say and look very upset, "you wouldn't offend an old friend, would you? If you don't have them they'll only go to waste and it would be wicked to waste such wonderful fruit, wouldn't it? Please accept them as a gift."

"Well, well," the old ladies would say and bob their heads. "We wouldn't offend you for anything, sir. We shall be honoured to accept such lovely fruit. Thank you muchly, sir."

The Misses Ponsonby's friend Mrs. Peploe had a Wool and Drapery shop a few doors away from the Tearoom. From behind the counter she would peer through skeins of wool. She looked like a sheep and I used to half expect her to baa. Mr. Peploe had been dead for many years; I never knew him, but he had been Rating Officer for the district and a Lay Preacher at the many Baptist Chapels in the locality — there was a strong non-conformist tradition in our area.

Like her friends the Misses Ponsonby, Mrs. Peploe had an abhorrence of drink, gambling, blood sports and vivisection. She collected money for the R.S.P.C.A. and painted not very good water colours of local scenes which her friends tried to sell in the Tearoom. Earlier I said that the Misses Ponsonby only left their shop to gather signatures for their petitions, but I was forgetting Sunday evenings when, accompanied by Mrs. Peploe, they walked to the Baptist Chapel for the evening service. Afterwards they could be seen chatting to dear Mr. Davies, the Minister, and other worshippers at the Chapel. They always referred to the Minister as "dear Mr. Davies, such a good man." Both Uncle George and I thought that all three of them were dear old ladies and every time that Uncle George killed a pig, there was always a nice piece of spare rib put aside to take to them, and they in turn invited Uncle George and me to supper occasionally. After we had eaten they would invite both of us to "take a little drop of something"; this was invariably ginger wine, kept especially for us, which they did not regard as an alcoholic drink. At Christmas, Uncle George always gave Mrs. Peploe and the Misses Ponsonby a small load of firewood. From Mrs. Peploe Uncle received either a pair of socks or mittens which she had knitted herself and from the Misses Ponsonby a selection of their jams, marmalades and jellies in neat little jars labelled in their copperplate script. Mrs. Peploe always gave me a pair of woollen gloves for Christmas and from the Ponsonby sisters I received a block of fudge which they made themselves.

Our groceries came from Mr. Gosworth's shop on the corner. Mother and Mrs. Gosworth were great friends, which is more than you could say about Mr. and Mrs. Gosworth. Mr. Gosworth was a tall thin man, very precise and fussy; Mrs. Gosworth nagged at the poor man, even in front of customers in the shop. "Yes dear, no dear, very good my dear, I'll do it as soon as I've served these customers," he'd say, but when he turned his head away I've noticed a nasty expression on his face. I sometimes thought that Mrs. Gosworth would go too far and then old Gosworth would do her in, perhaps strangle her with a cheese wire, or slice her up on his new bacon slicer.

At his Emporium, Mr. Pemberthy sold grocery and clothes. Most of the working men wore his corduroy, fustian or Derby tweed jackets, waistcoats and trousers. He also sold a special brand of hard wearing trousers which, when new, were as stiff as boards and, it was said, that when they were taken off they would stand up straight on the bedroom floor. Reuben Kimmins once said that when he had a pair of these his wife had woken in the night and, trembling, she clutched hold of Reuben and whispered, "There's a man standing by the bed!" But when Reuben looked he saw that it was only the stiff hardwearing trousers.

The Emporium sold thick flannel shirts and underwear and those large red spotted handkerchiefs, khaki smocks, strong blue overalls, big flat caps, cheap Trilby hats, mufflers and thick coarse socks. Timid Mrs. Pemberthy, who stood in awe of her domineering husband, sold a range of ladies' clothes in a separate room, cheap frocks, frumpy hats, serviceable underwear and hosiery.

Unlike the other traders, Mr. Pemberthy was a thrusting business man, "Competition is the life blood of trade, that's what I say," he often remarked, "S.P.Q.R. is my motto." A big notice outside the shop announced, "PEMBERTHY'S EMPORIUM FOR THE BEST VALUE ANYWHERE." He was always trying to undercut Gosworth's prices for sugar, bacon and cheese. Notices were stuck in his windows, "THE EMPORIUM HAS THE CHEAPEST BACON IN TOWN", (most people referred to the village as 'town'), "PEMBERTHY'S SUGAR PRICE CUT AGAIN".

If trade was slack he would stand outside his shop, shoulders hunched and chin pushed forward and when anyone approached he would shout, "The Emporium for bargains" and wringing his hands vigorously, "Now's the time to buy, prices slashed again." He often bought large stocks of shirts and trousers and reduced the price of them gradually week by week. "SHIRTS CHEAPER THIS WEEK" the notice in a window would announce. But he was never allowed to forget the time he put this large notice in the window, "PEMBERTHY'S TROUSERS DOWN AGAIN."

* * *

Mr. and Mrs. Gerrish kept the Post Office and Telephone Exchange and as Mrs. Gerrish worked the switchboard she was able to listen in to many an interesting conversation. Telegrams were delivered with the letters next day unless Mr. Gerrish considered them urgent, when he would saddle his pony and ride off to deliver them if it were any distance. Mrs. Gerrish was one of the few friends of Mother's who was also friendly with Uncle George; he often called at the Post Office for a chat and sometimes took Mrs. Gerrish half-a-dozen eggs, 'to keep her sweet.'

* * *

Edward Jones kept the garage. Apart from selling petrol he did motor and bicycle repairs and charged the accumulators for our wireless sets. He continuously had a cigarette in his mouth and was constantly coughing and spluttering. Cross-eyed and tiny, he was terrified of his large fat wife, but the big worry of his life was his twenty year old son. "I don't know what I'll do with our Bert, work

24

he wun't, and the only thing he do take an interest in is getting off with them hot-arsed wenches."

*   *   *

Mr. Bonnor Dawes bought milk from two local farmers and delivered it round the village. He was widely suspected of watering the milk, and the day he saw the Milk Inspector approaching he slipped and upset the two buckets of milk he was carrying. People said that this was no accident, but an example of how quickly Bonnor Dawes could act in an emergency.

*   *   *

Micah Elford had a fish and greengrocery shop up at Uncle George's end of the village. Two days a week he drove round in a small green van selling his goods. The customers on these rounds were expected to buy exactly what Elford offered them and if they refused more than twice Mr. Elford did not call again.

Apart from things like oranges, bananas and cucumbers, Micah Elford grew most of the fruit and vegetables he sold. He had one orchard adjoining Uncle George's and Uncle would watch him from his side of the hedge. One day we saw Elford watching a fowl of Uncle's who laid her eggs in the bottom of the hedge. The fowl, having laid her egg, walked off clucking, but Elford remained still, his eyes upon the place where the egg was laid.

"Hi there, Micah," shouted Uncle George, "that's my egg."

"I don't want your old egg," shouted Micah Elford.

"No, and I don't want yer stinkin' ole fish either," yelled back Uncle George.

And that about completes our list of shopkeepers, except for Father of course, who kept the hardware shop in the High Street.

Chapter 4

THE SCHOOL

ONE Saturday morning I was reading in bed — the book I remember, was *The Arabian Nights,* borrowed from school. The school had forty-seven pupils from the age of five to eleven years, Mrs. Simpkins, Headmistresss, and Miss Lockit, Assistant Teacher. As at most Church of England Schools at that period, we did get an awful lot of Religion and once a fortnight the Vicar visited us, and we looked forward to this as we did to the annual visit of the Religious Inspector. After the Inspector had talked to us and asked questions and we had sung, "There is a Green Hill Far Away," he handed out sweets to us all. But this was very different from our routine lessons of Religion with Mrs. Simpkins and Miss Lockit. The religious teaching which they drummed into us day after day only succeeded in making religion seem unwholesome and unclean.

However, to return to the Arabian Nights, as I lay there reading I heard an unusual noise. At first, I paid little attention to it, then the cacophony became louder and I became more alert. I'd heard a noise like this once before, I now recollected, that was the time when my ferret got in with Mother's Maran pullets. There had been a great deal of fuss about that and Mother declared that she would never again keep pullets to be murdered by such a vicious creature and I was made to get rid of the ferret, much to my secret delight. I had come to hate the thing, not that I'd ever let this be known. I'd only had the damned thing in the beginning because several of my friends had ferrets.

But now I could hear Mother's feet pounding up the stairs, the bedroom door flew open and there she stood, breathing heavily, her hair was awry, her face red and distraught and her eyes enlarged like they always were when she was upset. "Oh dear, oh dear," she said. "Why do you do it?" I lay there silently accepting the full blast of her anger. "Why do you do it?" she wailed. "I don't know whatever Father will say when he comes in to breakfast." She thrust a letter under my nose. "Look at this. This letter has just come from Mrs. Simpkins. Oh my poor dear boy — oh you wicked boy, oh that a son of mine could do such a thing. I don't know what Father will say. Oh dear, oh dear, the worry of it all. I think I shall go clean out of my mind."

With this, Mother rushed downstairs again, no doubt to get Father's breakfast ready and tell him the dreadful news. There was no mystery now, not as far as I was concerned. After the dreadful events of last Thursday afternoon Mrs. Simpkins had threatened to write to my parents, and, by God, she had, and made the most of it if Mother's behaviour was anything to go by. There had been a terrible todo on that Thursday and now there was more to come. Everyone made such a fuss and I was filled with shame.

My friends and I had acted with the best of motives, but Mrs. Simpkins hadn't seen it like that at all, which just goes to show how careful you should be, and how dangerous it is to try going about doing good. We had been plagued at school by a fat, bumptious, little girl called Bessie, for weeks past she had made our lives a misery. No matter what we did she found out about it, and our every move was related to Mrs. Simpkins. Worse still, if we didn't do anything, she did, and always managed to get us blamed as culprits. You'd scarcely credit the things she did and she would stand there looking up at Mrs. Simpkins, all wide-eyed innocence, while she told her convincing whoppers.

"We shall have to do something about her," said Ted.

"Yes, we'll teach her to tell tales," said Ronald.

Herbert looked quite venomous as he spoke. "She's making every day at school a downright misery, ole Simpky was bad enough before she started, but every day now we're being called out in front for something."

"We'll all have to think about it," I said.

We all agreed something would have to be done, but what?

After a lot of discussion on the way home one night, we all hurried over our tea and then met in an old tumbledown shed on Farmer Noakes' farm. We had each agreed to come from different directions, so as to be unnoticeable, and I was appointed to be there first and not to let anyone else in unless they said the password. As

Ronald said, "You can't be too careful on a job like this." When I arrived at the shed Ronald was already there waiting and Ted arrived a few minutes after me in a bit of a mess, his clothes torn and muddy. "I thought I saw somebody, so I jumped into a ditch to hide. You can't be too careful," he explained.

We waited silently for some minutes and then, tap, tap, tap, tap on the door, we could see through a chink in the wood that it was Herbert, but we let him go on tapping until he asked rather peevishly to be let in. "Say the password," we all hissed. "I can't, I've forgotten it" he muttered. Ronald crept out through a hole in the back of the shed to tell him the password again and I began to wish we had not included Herbert, it looked already as if he'd mess the whole job up.

We talked and talked about Bessie's past and present crimes and speculated on her future ones. We discussed other unpleasant aspects of Bessie. For one thing she smelt. "She wets her knickers," said Ted, "and when she gets near the stove she gives off vapours." "She's rude," said Herbert. "Do you know what my sister said?" Yes, yes, we all knew what Herbert's sister had said and of course we all wanted to hear and talk about it again. "She's too fat," I said, "she won't be a long liver — her grandfather should put her on a diet."

"That's it! that's it!" said Ronald. "It's her grandfather's job to teach her better ways; she lives with him and she's his responsibility."

"That's all very well," I said, "but he doesn't do anything."

"Well, he'll have to be told then, won't he?" went on Ronald.

"Who's going to tell him?" asked Ted.

"If nobody else will, then we must," replied Ronald.

"I'm cold and I want my supper," said Herbert.

"Do you think that will do any good?" I asked.

"The old fool will have to be made to face up to his duty," Ronald said.

"Coo, you ain't half in a mess Ted, you won't half get it when you get home," said Herbert.

We told Herbert to shut up; including him had definitely been a mistake.

"What we must do is put it in writing, people take more notice of the written word. My Father fr'instance don't take no notice of anything I tell him, but if he reads it in the paper, he won't half sit up," said Ronald.

We turned out our pockets and managed to produce a scrap of paper and a stub of pencil. "Here," Herbert said to me, "you write something. We'll all keep quiet while you have a think."

I sat over in a corner alone and chewed the pencil and eventually wrote in block letters, YAH YOUR GRANDDAUGHTER IS TOO

BIG FOR HER BOOTS YAH. I showed it to the others; they were impressed, I could see that.

"You've put that remarkably well," said Ted.

"That'll show him," said Herbert.

"That'll make the old fool sit up," said Ronald. "Now the lazy old toad will have to do something".

"Who's going to deliver it?" asked Ted.

Eeny, meeny, miney, mo; Herbert had to go.

Hidden behind the hedge, we watched Herbert poke the letter through the door. We had to watch Herbert, we could never be too sure of him. Herbert came scurrying down the path and joined us behind the hedge, his face was white and his hands were shaking. "What's the matter with you, Herbert?" we asked. "I'm cold and I'm hungry and I want my supper," he said.

We set off to our homes to supper convinced we'd done a good job. "Saved Bessie from the gallows most like," said Ted. Soon there would be a change for the better in Bessie. Our troubles in that quarter were over, we thought.

Nothing happened next day, nor the next. We didn't expect it to, the old grandfather must be given time. Nothing happened during that week — really it was too bad, that old grandfather was a lazy old toad, but even he ought to have done something by now. Bessie was worse if anything, perky and cocky and she contrived to give off more odious vapours. Mrs. Simpkin was daft to be taken in by her and Miss Lockit was no better.

Then on that terrible Thursday afternoon Mrs. Simpkins had a visitor, we didn't know who it was, because he or she was in the cloakroom. Then Bessie was called to the cloakroom. This is it, we thought. Bessie is for it at last.

Suddenly Mrs. Simpkins came back with the turkey look. She had the turkey look every morning as she sat with her back to the wall and played the piano. As she played she jerked her head backwards and forwards, and we all hoped that one morning she'd crack her head on the wall. But this afternoon she had a very nasty fierce turkey look and we all felt sorry for poor Herbert when she yanked him off to the cloakroom.

A few minutes later Ted was summoned into the cloakroom and soon after Ronald went and then it was my turn. The cloakroom wasn't very big and by the time I got in there it was a bit of a crush. In addition to Mrs. Simpkins, Bessie, Herbert, Ted, Ronald and I, there was Miss Lockit and old Grandfather. Miss Lockit with her black, beady, protruding eyes was giving a very passable imitation of a pekinese who'd seen something nasty in the woodshed, she gave a kind of yap from time to time, which helped her impression no end. Mrs. Simpkins was squawking like a turkey as well as looking like one. When I was young I seemed to be surrounded by adults who, when angry, looked like animals. However, I'm straying from the point. Over in the corner stood Bessie's old grandfather with his wet bleary eyes, his large nose with a dewdrop on the end of it, and his walrus moustache drooping like a flower without water. He just stood there, silent and twitching. Mind you, I reckon he'd had plenty to say earlier on. Bessie was quiet too, but smirking for all she was worth. Poor old Herbert shocked me, he was white and trembling and too far gone for speech, his head sagged and his eyes were sunk back in their sockets, his lip quivered and he kept giving loud sniffs, which was not very nice. Crikey, I thought, old Simpky and Locky haven't half been giving him some stick; they'd be had up if they did it to animals. It was all very well for that old grandfather to stand there like a dumb cluck, he must have told any amount of lies and made mischief in some order. Oh yes, it was very nice for him standing there, with his gaping mouth and watering eyes, I'll bet the old toad was enjoying every minute of it.

"Come on now," screamed Mrs. Simpkins to me, "I want the truth. Tell me the truth!"

I hung my head and said I knew nothing about anything. She then reeled off a list of our misdeeds, those we'd committed and those that Bessie had committed for us. She was particularly vindictive about the blocking of the school drains. I didn't think she need have brought that up again. We'd all been caned for it and that should have been enough, I thought, but she thought otherwise and was now on yet again about Ronald kicking her shin while she caned him.

"But this is the most serious of all the bad things you've done. Sending anonymous letters is a serious crime," she said. At the mention of anonymous letters I really got frightened. Recently I'd read Sexton Blake and the Poisonous Pen. The anonymous writer in that had had monkey glands, and ended up jumping off the church steeple — was this the sort of thing I was heading for?

Her next sentence increased my worry, "If I don't get the truth, I shall call in Police Detectives." I'd already made up my mind that when I left school I would become a detective, but my career would be ruined before it ever got started if I got on the wrong side of the police now. It had become hot and stuffy in the crowded cloakroom, the window was steamed up and Bessie was beginning to pong.

On and on went Mrs. Simpkins, she even remembered the time we'd got some of the infants squiffy on Uncle George's cider, and when we'd put pepper on the flowers causing Locky to sneeze out her false teeth. Let bygones be bygones, Uncle George always said, but these teachers loved raking up old scores. I wished I had the courage to say, 'Bury the axe'.

Eventually she returned to the letter and Locky gave yaps of encouragement; poor old Herbert was on the brink of tears, sniffing away like billy-ho. I'd had no intention of admitting to anything, but in the end I was so sick of the whole business that I confessed to writing the letter. The look of relief on poor Herbert's face made it seem worthwhile.

"I'll write to your parents, you wicked boy," said Mrs. Simpkins.

After old grandfather had left Mrs. Simpkins lined the four of us up in the classroom and squeaked to Miss Lockit, "Get the cane out of the cupboard, please, Miss Lockit." Simpky kept the cane for special occasions. Usually she rapped us over the knuckles with a ruler, but she never rapped Cedric Pollard but once, when he made a terrible racket, and his Mother came to school and made such a fuss that Cedric never got rapped again. I suppose Simpky thought the game wasn't worth the candle.

Anyway, she gave us all several whacks on our hands with the cane, and I noticed she stood well back when it came to Ronald's turn. Pity she didn't let old grandfather stop to see the caning, the cruel old toad would have enjoyed it.

On that Saturday morning, Father was sitting at the breakfast table with his bacon and eggs and Mrs. Simpkins' letter before him. I could tell he was angry, he had the bloodhound look — see what I mean about those adults and their animal expressions?

"Now then, boy, what's the meaning of all this you've been up to, eh?" he asked. "This sort of job has got to stop and damn quick too, or you'll be in prison. You're a downright wicked lad and your Mother's in a dreadful state. You ought to have your hide tanned, y'know."

"It's a disgrace to us all, I don't know how I'll be able to face Mrs. Simpkins," said Mother.

"We'd better send him to the Chapel School," said Father.

That's a good idea, I thought; I was right fed up with old

Simpky's school.

"Oh no we won't," said Mother. "Whatever would Mrs. Peabody say?"

Father picked up the *Daily Mail* and started to read it.

"It's all that George's fault," said Mother. "I knew it, I knew it, filling the boy's head up with all those tales. That talk of murder and those penny dreadfuls."

"There's no need to bring our George into it, Ethel." said Father. "You know I don't hold with all that book rubbish he reads, none on it's true. I can't understand him over that, he's such a level headed chap in other ways."

"Level headed! Soft headed if you ask me," said Mother.

"Now Ethel, I won't have you going on about our George like that."

"Going on, what about me after such goings on," said Mother. "As if George hasn't disgraced us enough, now there's this terrible business. I shall never be able to face Mrs. Simpkins again. I shall never be able to go to her Whist Drives at the school ever again, and she made the most delicious coffee, she brewed it for a fortnight. My social life is ruined and all because of that George."

Mother launched into a tirade about Uncle George and this was my salvation. Father thought a lot of Uncle George and if there was one sure way to rile him it was to say a word against his brother. Father's anger with me diminished, he knew that I, too, thought a lot of my Uncle and we became allies in his defence — my misdeeds forgiven or forgotten.

"They won't have the boy in the choir now," said Mother. "He don't want to be in the choir, and I don't know as I want him to be either," Father replied firmly. "If he spent his Sundays in church instead of in that George's company, this would never have happened," snapped Mother as she started gathering up the dirty crocks.

"If I were you," Father whispered to me, when Mother was at the sink, "I'd make myself scarce for the rest of the day. Go down to your Uncle and give him a hand with his pigs and garden."

Chapter 5

IT TAKES ALL SORTS...

MOST of the houses and shops in the village were stone built, though some were either of brick or plaster. In the narrow lanes which led off the High Street — we had several of these lanes, mainly cobbled, and most of them looped round to rejoin the main street — there were several half-timbered houses. A few of them had a brick base with an overhanging timbered upper storey.

But it was the church and its spire which dominated the whole village — we firmly believed it to be the most beautiful spire in all Gloucestershire. I could not imagine that a taller, more splendid spire could exist anywhere.

The Reverend Howard Bence had been the Vicar for more than twenty years, an elderly, tall, stooping man with a flowing mane of white hair. He was very short-sighted and wore pince-nez spectacles with a black cord attached to them. The spectacles were constantly falling off his long thin nose and dangling from the cord around his neck. Kindly and self-effacing, he gave the impression of vagueness, but in actual fact he was practical and alert, ever ready to give help, advice and comfort to those who needed it. Many troubles had been skilfully avoided or smoothed out by Mr. Bence who saw virtue in everybody. All in all, it was no wonder that we regarded Mr. Bence with affectionate respect.

Mrs. Lloyd and Mrs. Heckitt who lived in adjoining cottages, must have often strained the Vicar's good opinion of the human race. Mr. Lloyd and Mr. Heckitt worked on the railway and were the best of friends, but their wives quarrelled on the slightest pretext. The shared washing copper was the source of much acrimony. Mrs. Lloyd (mother of Herbert) would not clean out the ashes after she'd used the copper, so Mrs. Heckitt cleaned them out and tipped them on Mrs. Lloyd's back doorstep. Had it not been for the timely intervention of Mr. Bence, both women, it was said, would have come to blows.

Their current row was about the relative merits of electricity and mains water — we had neither in the village. Mrs. Heckitt wanted mains water and would not concede that electricity was of any use, while Mrs. Lloyd wanted electricity and regarded mains water as an abomination. I was in The Emporium one day and the two of them were going it hammer and tongs. "It's dark in here, Mr. Pemberthy," said Mrs. Lloyd. "What you want is electricity," and then louder, with a nasty sidelong look at Mrs. Heckitt, who was putting several large bars of soap in her basket, "What we all wants is electricity."

"That we don't, that we don't," snapped Mrs. Heckitt. "What we wants is main water."

"What nonsense some people do talk, Mr. Pemberthy," went on Mrs. Lloyd. "Everybody knows, every sensible body that is, that we wants electricity."

"Well . . ." said Mr. Pemberthy, not knowing what to say and certainly not wishing to appear to side with either customer.

"Exactly, Mr. Pemberthy, that's what I say, we've all got wells with water in 'em, what do we want with mains water?"

"They're dry half the summer," muttered Mrs. Heckitt.

"That's 'cos some do squander water. Washing, washing, all the time, 'tis unnecessary," retorted Mrs. Lloyd.

"I do like it sanitary, I do like it sanitary, Mr. Pemberthy," said Mrs. Heckitt, her voice rising to a shriek.

"And I like it light," came back Mrs. Lloyd.

"You don't know what you're talking about," said Mrs. Heckitt.

"Stuff and nonsense, that mains water is harmful — they put chemicals in it. We should all get tumours."

"I want plenty of water because I like to keep everything sanitary."

"Electricity has got dozens of uses, as you know, Mr. Pemberthy. We should hold a public meeting and demand electricity," said Mrs. Lloyd.

"I b'lieve the woman's gone off her head Mr. Pemberthy," said Mrs. Heckitt.

"What's that? What's that?" screamed Mrs. Lloyd, "You heard what she called me, Mr. Pemberthy. I'll have the law on her I will, you heard what she said, Mr. Pemberthy?"

"I heard nothing Mrs. Lloyd," said Mr. Pemberthy. "I've got a bit hard of hearing of late, I shall have to go and see Dr. Higgins about it."

"I like it sanitary," screamed Mrs. Heckitt.

"And I want electricity," screeched Mrs. Lloyd.

They were still hard at it when I left.

I don't know how Mrs. Lloyd's and Mrs. Heckitt's neighbours, Mr. and Mrs. Fowler, put up with the shouting and brawling. Emmanuel Fowler and his wife were the quietest, the most peaceful, and the most respectable people. Emmanuel, a man in his thirties, was a clerk at Mr. Farquharson's and a sidesman at Church. His wife was a member of the Mothers' Union and Secretary of the Women's Institute. Their two young children were tidy, clean and well behaved, and they attended Sunday School regularly. Uncle George said that working up at old Farquharson's would drive Emmanuel Fowler round the bend sooner or later, it was never natural for any man to be so good, so peaceful and so servile. I thought Mrs. Lloyd and Mrs. Heckitt would do the same for poor Mrs. Fowler. Uncle and I used to talk about it sometimes and we were of the opinion it was a most unwholesome life for them and that one day there'd be hell to pop.

Dr. Higgins' house and surgery were not far from the Church. Dr. Higgins, a bluff, down to earth man, was on good terms with everyone, calling most people by their first names. Father said that it didn't matter how ill you felt, as soon as Dr. Higgins arrived at the house you felt better. He must have made many visits without any hope or expectation of payment, but I don't suppose he ever gave it a thought.

Dr. Higgins was a keen fishing and shooting man and the only time he was a bit testy was when his assistant was busy elsewhere and he was called to a patient just when he was preparing to set off on a shooting or fishing expedition. Uncle George, though faithful to his patent medicines, had a high opinion of Dr. Higgins, pronouncing him, 'first class,' or 'A.1.'

*　　*　　*

Major Mostyn was a regular visitor to Uncle George on Sunday mornings. He came to buy eggs and usually stopped to inspect the gardens and drink a mug of cider. "It's absolutely marvellous, the wonderful stuff you produce in your garden, George; I can't get anything much to grow in mine."

"And no bloody wonder," Uncle George would remark after he'd gone, "with them great spotted dogs his missus have got scambling all over it."

*　　*　　*

Ronald Ferneyhough was a carpenter and undertaker. He was a small sallow-looking man and Uncle George said he would snoop around the district and pubs to see if he could spot anyone who looked like dying. If he did, he would study them and make notes of their measurements in a little book he carried in a waistcoat pocket.

We had two sawmills in the vicinity and most of the local men worked there or on farms, apart from those who had jobs on the railway or, like Amos Bloxham, worked on the road. Amos, a tall, gaunt, dour man was married to a woman very much younger than himself. He suspected she was having a 'carry-on' with various men while he was away at work. There wasn't, as far as we knew, any evidence that she was, but the absence of evidence didn't allay Amos' suspicions, it only increased them, and he was convinced in his own mind that she was 'carrying on'. Women were deceivers, in his opinion, and that was that. He only had to see her go into The Emporium to exclaim, "Oho, so that's the way it is, is it? Pemberthy's her fancy man now then. Oho, oho, so he's her fancy man. So the dirty hussy's carrying on with Pemberthy now, is she? I never did trust the man, I could see what he was by his eyes."

If he saw his wife out walking while he was working on the road, he'd say to his workmates, "Thur goes my wife, a cockin' her arse to every man she sees."

Near the Church was a rather grand Georgian house, the home and offices of Mr. Farquharson, solicitor. We saw little of him in the village, he remained aloof and dignified. He must have been a great age, for he looked brittle as bones and dry as dust. Presumably some of the local people had business with him, but on the few occasions I

36

saw him he seemed to ignore everyone, certainly he never spoke to me, and I stood in awe of so venerable a figure.

Uncle George certainly wasn't in awe of him however, he had no great opinion of him and made no secret of it. Once, when Alfred Tucker had to appear at court with Mr. Farquharson to defend him, Uncle said, "Well, Alfred, may the Lord help you, 'cos old Farquharson wun't."

* * *

On past Mr. Farquharson's in a dilapidated house lived old Mr. Pontifex, who was reputed to be a professor. Music was his great passion. When passing his house one could often hear the sound of his piano. Ever since the death of his wife many years ago he had lived alone, refusing to allow another woman to enter the house. When Uncle George had the bakery I often used to deliver bread to him and got to know him well. Uncle still called there once or twice a week, I think to make sure that the old gentleman was all right, and I sometimes accompanied him.

Though the old gentleman's house and person were exceedingly dirty, his manner was charming. He treated everyone in the most courteous way. His voice was rich and cultured and the expression on his grimy face was benign. Whenever we visited him, he invited us inside and gave each of us a glass of very dry sherry.

Afterwards as we walked down the long path through his wilderness of a garden, Uncle would say, "Dirty he may be, eccentric perhaps, but he's what I call a proper toff."

* * *

Casper Rochester was a 'mystery man'. Mrs. Gerrish said he was a 'remittance man', a member of a well known aristocratic family who sent him a weekly postal draft with the condition that he kept away. The remittance must have been substantial because, though he did not work, he could afford to spend most of his time drinking in The Rose and Crown. He was a big, powerful man and, when drunk, he could be a bit of a handful. On such occasions Trophimus Ellicot, the landlord, sent for the policeman.

P.C. Cardew, captain of the cricket team and champion shove-halfpenny player, handled the drunken Mr. Rochester with great tact. "Come along, Mr. Rochester, sir, you've had a hard day, come on now and I'll give you a hand home. I want you in bed early tonight because I'm relying on you for tomorrow's match." And Mr. Rochester would go meekly off home with him. P.C. Cardew could handle him all right, but nobody else could. I think the fact that they were both keen cricketers helped.

The Rose and Crown was our largest public house and was always referred to as 'the hotel' because they had accommodation for visitors. During the summer months they had quite a few people to stop there, it being a convenient place from which to explore our lovely and interesting countryside. During the winter it was cold, wet and muddy, but from the time the plum blossom appeared until the fall of the year, our locality was enchanting – no wonder our native poet called it, 'this sweet shape of land and winding river'.

We had people of all ages stopping at the hotel; elderly people who enjoyed the peace and quiet; botanists – our woodlands provided them with plenty of interest; geologists – we have rocks of more geological periods than anywhere else in Britain; middle aged couples, and families; and young people. The latter always gave rise to much talk between Mother and her friends. They were amused to see grown men wearing shorts; scandalised by young women wearing either trousers or very short shorts, their faces often heavy with make-up and smoking cigarettes in the street. And shocked to hear of women drinking beer in the tap-room.

Uncle George soon became friendly with some of these visitors and would invite them to see his pigs, his garden and orchards. They made a great fuss of Uncle, and enjoyed sitting in his garden shed sipping his home made wine and cider. Mother made caustic remarks about these summer friendships and said, "It's downright disgusting, that old George prancing about with those scantily clad young flibberty-gibbets." Not that Uncle George took the slightest notice of her when she told him about it to his face. "There's no harm in our George," Father told her.

"No man's to be trusted as far as women are concerned," Mother said.

"Our George has never been interested in women," Father replied.

"What about Mrs. Williams? Beetroot, pictures, chocolates and all that?"

"That will be quite enough," said Father.

*   *   *

The White Lion was Uncle George's favourite pub and this was where all the railwaymen went too, the porters, the signalmen and the gangers. Our Railway Station stood about a mile out of the village and when visitors asked why the station was so far away, our stock answer, which we thought rather clever, was, "Because that's where the railway is."

There must be something about the railway which makes men who work on it take to gardening, because all the railwaymen I've known have been keen gardeners. Our railwaymen and Uncle George gathered at The White Lion to discuss gardening. Between the railwaymen and Uncle George there was a friendly rivalry quite unlike the rivalry between Uncle and Fred Pollard, the jobbing gardener. Pollard fancied himself as a prize gardener and could never accept the fact that Uncle was much the better of the two.

From July to November the bar of The White Lion was festooned with prize vegetables. Someone would bring in a long runner bean which Arnold Ludgater would hang up on the shelves behind the counter. Then someone else would bring in another, perhaps half an inch longer, then another a shade longer still, until there was a whole row of them. Carrots, shallots, onions, potatoes would be brought to be exhibited on the shelves and when all available shelf space was filled, the windows would be used to display the vegetables which would soon be accompanied by apples and pears. Big marrows and pumpkins were a problem and Ludgater limited the display to three of each only and a table would be used for them. There was a piano there and on Saturday nights, if I walked past The Lion, I could hear the music and people singing. I've no doubt that Uncle George often told the tale of the man who swallowed the wheelbarrow at The Lion one hot summer evening, many years ago.

* * *

From all accounts, there was never anything jolly going on at the third pub, The Bull, certainly no music or singing. Cratchley, the landlord, was reputed to have shares in the brewery which owned all three pubs, and because he had shares it was rumoured that his beer was stronger. The rumour was never confirmed or denied, but it did not attract many customers.

Uncle George said it was dark, gloomy and miserable there and the customers were mainly old cronies of Cratchley's, "moaners, trouble makers and liars." Cratchley was a widower (it was said he had worked and bullied his wife to death) and late in the evenings he would be drunk. When drunk, he would alternatively cry and recite religious texts. "He's got plenty to cry about, the old varmint," said Uncle George, "He's that wicked, I can't understand why that wooden leg of his hasn't gone rotten."

* * *

"Don't get talking to that Gert," was a frequent warning I had from my Mother. Dirty Gerty all the villagers called her, but Uncle George often stopped and had a chat with her. "Gert," I heard him say to her once, "You're a dirty, lewd, drunken, immoral woman. Here's half-a-crown, go and get some stout down you."

She spent every shilling as fast as she got it, saying "Might as well blew the bugger, as hoard'n up". If she had a little windfall, she'd spend the lot at the jug and bottle of one of the pubs. When nicely drunk, she'd dance up the High Street, dirty ragged skirt held high, chanting at the top of her voice, "I don't give a damn, that's the sort of gal I am, Anybody can have a bit, if they've a mind to pay, Sunday, Monday, any bloody day."

As Uncle George said, it takes all sorts to make a world.

Chapter 6

GOOD FRIDAY MORNING

"YOU sure you won't come after all, Ethel?" asked Father.

"No, I'm certainly not coming, I'm going to church with Mrs. Gosworth," replied Mother.

"It's well worth seeing, Ethel, make up your mind," said Father.

"I've made up my mind thank you very much," said Mother.

"You'd enjoy the drive, it's a pretty bit of country."

"I wouldn't like risking my neck with that George driving."

"Don't be like that, Ethel, not on a Good Friday."

"Be like what?" asked Mother.

"Nasty gritted about our George. You'd enjoy the change of air, down on the Severn it's like sea air," said Father.

"I shouldn't enjoy the smell of beer fumes on the way back."

"The Severn Bore's a wonderful sight, we're lucky to be living so close; it comes up with a rushing sound."

"I get enough bore all the year round with George everlasting here."

"You never miss a chance to be nasty about our George," said Father. "You sure you won't come?"

"I'm quite sure thank you," answered Mother. "I've arranged to go to church with Mrs. Gosworth."

"Well, please yourself. We must get off or we'll miss it. Our George is out there waiting for us."

I got into the back seat of Uncle George's Ford Eight and Father sat in the front with Uncle.

41

"Ethel isn't coming then?" asked Uncle George.

"No, she didn't feel up to it, and besides, she felt she'd better go to church with Mrs. Gosworth — she always goes with her on a Good Friday and she felt Mrs. Gosworth would be offended if she didn't go with her to-day. Mind, she wanted to come. She didn't say anything, but I could see she was upset about missing the trip," lied Father.

"A pity," said Uncle George.

"Ah, it were a pity," said Father.

"Another time perhaps," said Uncle George.

"Ah, another time perhaps."

It was downhill all the way and Uncle George leaned well back in his seat.

"Nice bunch of bullocks out there," said Uncle, pointing.

"Just look at those daffodils out in that wood. Ethel'd liked to have seen that," said Father, a few moments later.

"It's nice to have Good Friday free," said Uncle George. "How I used to have to work with them hot cross buns!"

"They was damn good buns, George, damn my rags if they weren't."

"Wonder what Banstead's buns'll be like, not much bottle I shouldn't wonder."

"Have he still got them two women living with him, George?"

"Ah, still got the two of 'em."

"Still got 'em, has he? Damned bad principled way of going on."

"Man's a damned fool."

"Daresay you're right, George."

"Wonder if the two women do quarrel?"

"All women do quarrel, George."

We passed a poultry farm and Father said, "See all them new poultry drinkers out there, George? Mrs. Turpin had them off me only last week, and ordered a dozen rolls of poultry netting. I told her I'd knock a fair bit off the wire as she was having a dozen rolls. Gave her a smart bit of divi on the drinkers for spot cash — she weren't half pleased. Damn good payers the Turpins, they're the kind of customers I like," said Father.

"Ah, it saves a terrible lot of work booking," said Uncle George.

"Ah, and it's cash in hand. Damn good payers the Turpins, pays to give 'em a good divi — always give you the ready — different from some baggers I've got on my books."

"Ah, some on 'em'll never pay."

"You're right there, George, there's some damn bad baggers about — and I've got some on 'em on my books."

"Some wettish old country down here," said Uncle. "Don't know as I'd like to farm it."

"Dare say you're right, George."

"Rajah rhubarb! There's a fellow there's got his taters up. They'll get cut off by the frost."

The countryside was different now, tall elm trees, orchards of plums and Bramley apples. The grass verges on either side of the road were sprinkled with celandines and dandelions, and cow parsley leaves were beginning to shoot. We turned into a narrow road with high hedges, we were now quite close to the river. A little later as we rounded a bend I saw mud on the road.

"Damn my rags George, the tide's been over here," said Father, very excited.

"Soak me bob, you're right, begod," answered Uncle.

"Must've bin a high one to come right over here, George."

"Must'a bin, the road's devilish slick."

"Better drive steady, George, don't want any mishaps. We should never hear the last of it from Ethel," warned Father.

"Don't you fear none, I'm a very skilful driver on a bit of slick road," reassured Uncle.

"Better pull in by the next gateway, George."

Uncle parked the car in the gateway and we had to climb over the gate which was tied up with wire. "Chap needs a set of gate irons," said Father. "I could let him have some worth the money."

We walked across the meadow, the river was hidden by the high bank built up alongside it.

"Nice bit of sun, I must get on with the garden," said Uncle.

"Lovely weather," agreed Father.

"These river meadows are no bloody good for three parts of the year," said Uncle George, "but rajah rhubarb, won't they throw up some kip during the summer months, if they don't get too many high tides. They get too much deposit of salt, and too much salt don't do the grass any good — make mushrooms grow though."

"By gum, it's wet out here, George."

Uncle George turned to me and said, "Well, boy, you've been quiet. I don't think you've said a word since we left. Enjoying yourself?"

"Oh yes, Uncle," I said.

"Soon see the river now," said Uncle.

"The Severn and the Wye, two of England's biggest rivers," said Father.

"Happy is the man who doth lie, twixt Severn and Wye," quoted Uncle in his fruity voice.

"Are we happy, I wonder?" mused Father.

"Happy as the day is long, ben't us, boy?" laughed Uncle. I smiled and nodded my head in answer.

We climbed the earth flood wall and saw the Severn.

"Rajah rhubarb!" said Uncle.

"More like a sea than a river," said Father.

The far bank was more than a quarter of a mile away, the water was deep and muddy, unlike the Wye whose water was clear enough to see its comparatively shallow bed.

"More like a sea," said Uncle George.

"I never did like the water," said Father. "The Wye frightens me, something dark and sinister about it, and all those rocks. Can't understand Dr. Higgins being so fond of fishing in it."

"Sport, that's what it is, gets a hold of a man."

"Never could understand sport, George, wading about in the cold water, or walking miles just to carry a gun."

"Never had the time to take it up," said Uncle.

"Never could understand sport, George. Still there's more sense in fishing and shooting – there is something on the end of it if you're lucky, but cricket and football are a damn fool of a job. Grown men hitting a ball about or chasing it over a muddy field – it's damn kiddish."

"Hush!" said Uncle "Here she comes."

We could hear a great roar rushing towards us and in a second we saw a head of water "Rajah rhubarb!" said Uncle. "Rajah rhubarb!"

"Stand back, stand back!" yelled Father.

"Her's six foot high, soak me bob if her ain't."

"What d'you think of that?" Father asked me when it had passed, the river still swollen with water.

"I've seen bigger ones in my time," said Uncle. "You've got to have a good wind to have a really high one."

"Good job it wasn't any higher this morning, George, or the lot on us would have been drowned," said Father.

We wiped our muddy boots on some thick clumps of grass by the hedge and got back into the car. Uncle drove along the lane until we came to a little pub called The Sloop. "We'll stop here and have a drink," he said. "The beer here is first class." Uncle and Father went into the pub and I sat on a wooden bench outside. Uncle brought me out a glass of lemonade and a bag of crisps and said the beer was A.1.

A man was selling elvers at the pub and Uncle and Father bought three pints of elvers apiece. Our Gloucestershire poet F. W. Harvey called elvers,

"Little wormy fish,
Chewed – string fish,
Slithery dithery fish."

We got back into the car and drove off.

"There's nothing like a good feed of elvers," said Uncle. "No," agreed Father. "There's nothing like a good feed of elvers."

On the way back Father said, "This have bin a good little car, George. I've been thinking of getting a little van to go round with my wares."

"Pig powders," said Uncle George.

"What?" said Father.

"Pig powders I said, you ought to sell pig powders and such, there's a call for 'em," explained Uncle.

"Metal wheelbarrows be all the go now," said Father.

"So they might be, but I'd sooner have a wooden barrow, old Felix used to make some wonderful pretty wooden barrers. Remember when old Zachary swallowed his'n at The Lion?"

"Ah," said Father, "we had some laughs in those days. The boy here'll never see such things as we saw, George."

"Never be the same again. Times be changed," said Uncle leaning forward as we went up hill.

Back home Mother had the dinner waiting for us, bacon and turnip greens. After Father had eaten a few mouthfuls he said, "That's some lovely turnip greens you brought, George." And Uncle replied, "Do your blood good."

"We've brought some elvers back, Ethel," said Father. "Cook some for our tea, George'll be here."

"Cook them yourself, I can't stand the sight of them," said Mother.

"Cook 'em with some of that fat bacon George brought, Ethel," said Father.

"All right, I'll do that," she said.

"Goodish ole Bore," said Uncle.

"Did you enjoy the service?" asked Father.

"Yes, Mrs. Peabody excelled herself on the organ," said Mother.

"Bet old Peabody rushed straight off to The Bull as soon as it was over," chuckled Uncle.

"I don't know where Mr. Peabody went," said Mother.

"He'll be drunk and snoring this afternoon," said Father.

"It's not true," snapped Mother.

"We saw a wood full of wild daffodils this morning," Father told her.

"The windflowers should be out in the spinney by now," said Uncle George. "It'll still be a bit damp underfoot though. Old Mother Peabody wants to mind she don't get her arse wet."

"Oh!" gasped Mother and left the room.

Chapter 7

OF PERSONS, PIGS, CABBAGES AND THINGS

UNCLE George's house had been the home of his parents. He, Father and their sister, Agnes, had been born and brought up there. Since the death of his Mother, long before I was born, Uncle had lived there alone and Aunt Aggie went once a week to tidy up a bit and give a quick flick round with a duster. Aunt Aggie was younger than Uncle George, but older than Father, and quite unlike either of them in looks or temperament. Her face was thin, aquiline, her eyes were hooded and her body was tall, gaunt, almost to the point of emaciation. Her clothes hung on her in folds and she looked and dressed either as if she were going to, or coming from, a funeral. Her dark, sombre, old fashioned clothes never varied winter or summer. To her, life was just one long complaint. If ever anyone had been needed to announce the end of the world Aunt Aggie would have been the ideal candidate.

Her husband, Sam Fisher, was a decorator and not a very good one either, by all accounts. Mother wasn't on speaking terms with Aunt Aggie ever since Uncle Sam had last done some decorating for us. Mother told Mrs. Peabody and Mrs. Gosworth (and I daresay quite a few others) what a botched-up job he'd made of it and Aunt Aggie got to hear. Aunt Aggie wouldn't hear a word said against her husband, and as most people had said a good few words against Sam Fisher, that explains why there were so many people Aunt Aggie 'wasn't speaking to'.

Anyway, down comes Aunt Aggie one evening and she and Mother had a right 'set-to'. Afterwards Father said, "As soon as I saw our

Aggie come to the door, I knew she'd come for a barney. She always were nasty tempered. I'll warrant she do give poor old Sam cause to chew that old moustache of his."

The row didn't last long, but while it did it was bitter, even Mrs. Lloyd and Mrs. Heckitt could have learnt a thing or two. Aunt Aggie's parting shot to Father when she got to the door was, "I never could understand what you could see in that great ungainly Ethel, she always did have too much to say even as a girl, and what a sloppy uncouth girl she was too."

After that, Aunt Aggie was never mentioned in our house.

Sam Fisher was a kind of male counterpart. He, too, was tall, gaunt and dismal. He had large red rimmed eyes and a huge handlebar moustache, he was slow moving and folks said he was lazy. "Come day, go day, any day'll do day," they called him. He didn't smoke, but sucked acid drops continuously, which perhaps accounted for the sour look on his face. He was supposed to be a teetotaler, but was, I heard, a secret drinker. Aunt Aggie could put a fair drop of drink away and her face made no secret of it either.

Uncle Sam rode a bicycle, slowly, very slowly, to wherever he happened to be working, with paint pots and brushes strapped to the carrier at the back and dangling and clanging from the handlebars. If anyone said, "Good-morning," or "How d'ye do," he dismounted and answered in a drawl, "It ain't a very good marning, no, not as far as I'm concerned it ain't. No, for one thing me back's bad again, I oughtn't to be a working today, not in my condition I oughtn't; but you know me, I never give up, never complain, just keep a'goin'." And if it wasn't his back it was his head, "Terrible bad 'eads I do get, I'm in agony with me 'ead agen this marnin'. I be a martyr to bad 'eads; I oughtn't to be a workin' today, not with a 'ead like I got."

Uncle Sam fancied himself as a singer of comic songs and would insist on singing them at our village concerts. He wasn't a good singer and as Uncle George said, "If there's one thing old Sam's worse at than decorating, it's singing comic songs. I'm afraid the chap's no bottle, no bottle at all, but our Aggie do seem to like'n."

Uncle George's house wasn't a particularly attractive house, but it was substantial, and that is what counted with my family. 'Substantial' was the supreme virtue and not only of houses, but of people too. If my father described anyone as 'substantial', he was bestowing his highest praise on them. But to return to the house. In the centre of the large kitchen stood a pinewood table, its top covered with black and white checked oil cloth, its legs painted brown and around this were four Windsor chairs, also painted brown, whilst against the wall stood a Welsh Dresser and chest of drawers, also painted brown, making the plain pinewood chest of drawers, with large brass handles, look startlingly bright. To one side of the large kitchen range stood a fine old walnut Windsor armchair. On the high mantelpiece over the range was a brass letter rack overflowing with letters; some china ornaments, a few bottles of pills, a tea-caddy, an old fashioned match holder and usually a couple of Uncle's pipes. Above all this hung a brown framed mirror, in which Uncle sometimes passed the time pulling faces.

There were a couple of other rooms, which were rarely used and of course the pantry, really quite a large, stone-flagged room, decked with shelves, where Uncle kept his provisions and china. The bacon was hung here, there was bacon hanging from hooks everywhere, you could scarcely move without banging your head on sides, or part sides, of bacon. Uncle George killed two pigs a year, one in late autumn and another in early spring, and as he never considered a pig fit to kill unless it was well over twenty score, he had far more bacon than he could possibly eat. He hacked away at the fat salty sides until they became too hard, rancid and yellow even for him to eat, then he'd abandon that side and start on another, but the abandoned sides were always left hanging to yellow and moulder. You are bound to be wondering why he killed two pigs a year if so much was allowed to go to waste, but Uncle would have denied they were wasted — there they were, still hanging there — if he'd thrown them away, now that would have been waste.

The reason he killed two pigs a year was because he'd always killed two pigs, like his Father before him, and Uncle would have thought he was lowering himself to have cut down to one pig — he'd be no better than a cottager. Secondly, Uncle George loved pig meat and offal, he was a glutton for faggots, chitterlings and the like (said Mother).

Upstairs was the bathroom where Uncle George kept most of his medicines. All the water had to be pumped to the overhead storage tank by hand, so he used the water sparingly. Then there were two bedrooms which were never used, and Uncle's bedroom. He had a four poster bed, a wardrobe, chest of drawers, an ottoman and a cane seated chair and small table. During the winter months Uncle 'boarded up' his bed to keep out draughts, leaving one side just low enough for him to climb in.

Soon after he had sold the bakery business he was able to buy the orchard and paddock he had coveted for so long. He bought extra stock; half a dozen Gloucester Old Spot gilts ("there's nurn a finer breed"), to increase his herd of breeding pigs and a Large White boar whom he called Brutus. He purchased ten yearling Hereford cattle ("they'm fine doers, them Herryfuds"); a hundred more Rhode Island Red Pullets ("they lay a beautiful brown egg"), and two new poultry-houses from Father to house them.

With the help of Reuben he erected another pig house in the corner of the orchard near Micah Elford's. "Thee casn't put hens up there, cast? Not near old Micah's boundary, he'd be tempted to help himself to an egg or two when he had a mind. I haven't forgotten how he eyed that hen of mine in the hedge. But even he couldn't help himself to a pig, not even a little 'un, cos I should hear the pig squeal and be atter him like a long dog."

Oh, and the bees; Uncle had had three hives of bees for some time. He wasn't a first class bee-keeper, he wouldn't have said so himself I'm sure, but he kept the bees to pollinate the orchards, and for the honey. He was inordinately fond of honey and claimed that it had great medicinal qualities. Even the stings, and he had a great many of them, were of value, he said. Nevertheless, he shouted and swore when he was stung. "But Uncle, if the stings are so good for you, why are you so angry?" I asked one day. A reasonable question I thought, but Uncle bellowed through his black veil, "Dazzed and set it, boy, because they do hurt summat cruel, that's why. Sometimes I wonder if you're as bright as you might be." Then he turned back to his bees muttering, "Rajah rhubarb, what a damn fool of a question." A bee must have stung him again, because he began shouting and swearing yet again.

"Why," I asked him when he'd finished and calmed down, "do you keep bees?" "Because," he chuckled, "they're the only livestock which can wander anywhere without anyone being able to kick up a bother." However, he wasn't much of a bee-keeper, more of a bee-loser really – his bees were always swarming. And Uncle George in straw hat and veil would be running all over the parish banging a tin tray. The banging of the tin tray was supposed to attract the escaping bees, or cause them to settle, but it never seemed to be very effective. Uncle George wasn't built for running about on hot summer days, clad in veil and long white gloves. It certainly gave Mother a further reason to be caustic at poor Uncle's expense. Usually she made her remarks at tea-time, while pouring Father's tea. "I saw that George rushing through the village in his fancy dress and banging his silly tin tray again this afternoon, everybody was tittering about it. The children were just coming out of school and even they were laughing about it. I'm that ashamed that I'm anything to do with him."

"He's after his bees again, Ethel, you know that as well as I do. But I must say it worries me, he'll have a heart attack rushing about on these hot afternoons. I wish he'd stop it," said Father.

"Huh," snorted Mother, "He can stop it alright – as soon as The White Lion opens. He's a bee fool, that's what he is."

"Now, now, Ethel, don't be like that about our George, he's a good living man," pleaded Father.

"Good living!" said an astonished Mother. "Good living you said? He's like a heathen dervish when he gets going on that tin tray. The other night, we'd just finished singing Jerusalem at our W.I. Meeting and the President was just about to introduce our Guest Speaker, when he rushes past, bang, bang, bang, on that wretched tray of his, and shouting some not very nice words – words I couldn't repeat. I go all hot at the thought of those words even now. I sat there petrified, I could feel my face go red, and all my friends sitting there too, and the President and the Guest Speaker – ooh, I prayed the ground would open and swallow me up – I shall never be able to hold my head up at a W.I. Meeting ever again. Every time we sing Jerusalem I shall think of it and be wondering if he'll come past banging and swearing. Nobody said anything about it, that made it all the worse somehow. They knew who it was and they all felt so sorry for me."

Mother paused for breath, Father and I said nothing.

"And if it isn't that George prancing about banging that tin tray, it's that dreadful great Sam Fisher, the sawney fool, cycling up and down the street jangling his paint pots. Whoever employs the great fool must be out of their minds. I shall never forget as long as I live that dreadful botched up job he did here. Thank goodness my family are respectable — I must have been mad in my head ever to have married into such a family as yours. No wonder Dorothea doesn't come to stay very often."

"Just pour me another cup of tea please, Ethel," said Father.

Dorothea was Mother's sister. She was married to a Bank Manager and lived near London. She came to stop for a few days in the summer and Mother was pleased to see her come, but not so pleased as I was to see her go. She fussed and swanked and nagged at me and crit, crit, crit all the time. I ought to do this, I should be made to do that, or I should be stopped from doing this and that — mainly having anything at all to do with Uncle George.

She said Uncle George was a low, common, good for nothing man, and Uncle thought she was a "funny bitch", and though Father didn't actually say so, I think this was his opinion too, and it was certainly mine.

I found it better to leave Uncle George alone when he was engaged on anything to do with his bees. Worst of all was honey extraction time, though now he had a proper extractor it was better than when he had tried to extract it by putting it through the mangle. Even Uncle was forced to admit that "there was bloody honey everywhere," and Aunt Aggie screamed blue murder when she came to tidy up.

So, when Uncle was busy with the bees on fine summer evenings, I went fishing with Tom, down at the lake. It wasn't a real lake, more of a big pool overhung by huge pollard willows, on Farmer Noakes' farm at the bottom end of the village. Moorhen and wild duck nested there, tench, huge carp and roach lived in the water. We rarely saw a tench, they stopped deep down in the mud at the bottom, and the carp were too wily to be caught, but the roach were comparatively easy to be lured with our bait of breadcrumbs. The lake had eels too; we would see them jumping up and out of the water and flopping back in again. Big fellows they were, but they wouldn't look at the lobworm we used to try and tice them with.

Gert was often sitting at the waterside with rod and line. She was a much more successful fisher than we were. Every few minutes she'd land a roach and each time she caught one she'd cackle. She took them home to cook and eat and before we left we gave her the ones we had caught. She would remain there after us, a forlorn, lone figure. Sometimes she would, apart from cackling when she caught a fish, sit there silently, occasionally laying her rod aside while she rolled a cigarette. Stansfield tobacco was what she smoked and the acrid smoke would drift towards us.

At other times she would talk to us, a few sentences now and again — Mother was never told of these meetings with Gert. It was Gert who taught Tom and me to catch roach. "You must strike immediately you feel or see a bite, as soon as the float moves — strike! Never let your eyes stray from the float or the fish will take the crumbs and be gone."

Once she told us she'd been on the stage. "I was Principal Boy in Pantomime many a time, the men would stand at the stage door waiting for me as I came out," — she paused, looked at us, her dirty crushed 'roll-up' smouldering at the corner of her mouth. "Aah, I can see you boys don't believe me — you see a dirty, untidy, drunken old woman, but once I was young and beautiful. I had talent too, but — well, never mind, it's a long time ago and what's past and gone is best forgotten."

She stared sadly and dreamily into the water. I felt as if I wanted to cry. Why was it all the people I liked best (and despite Gert's reputation and Mother's strictures, I liked Gert) had an underlying sadness about them, although on the surface, they were the jolliest of people. Mr. Teakle, the two Misses Ponsonby, Mrs. Peploe, Mr. Pontifex, even Uncle George, had that something, not that they ever said so, it would have been out of character for any of them ever to complain, least of all Uncle George, but some instinct told me it was there.

Gert recited, more to herself than to Tom and me,

"I feel like one
Who treads alone
Some banquet-hall deserted,
Whose lights are fled,
Whose garlands dead,
And all but he departed!"

She looked up, turned to us and said with a smile — like a flash of defiance, "There's life in this gal yet. Never despair, never give up, fight and laugh to the bitter end. They can't get a good laugher down — and I've had some laughs in my time. I ain't done for yet and I'll bang about 'til I drop."

*   *   *

We had a penchant for grandiose names. We called the village, the town; The Rose and Crown, the Hotel; the big pool, the lake. And not only places but people too, the Chairman of the Parish Council was the Mayor. Similarly, we called Mr. Biggs the Colonel, even his wife called him Colonel, he'd been called Colonel for so long that most people had probably forgotten what his first name was. We particularly liked giving military titles to people, sometimes because they seemed apt. The station master, because of his gold braided cap and uniform and the way he strutted up and down the station platform, was called General, but I have no idea why Mr. Biggs (who had risen no higher than Lance Corporal during the Great War) was called Colonel.

Colonel called at our home at least once a week, not to buy anything in the hardware line, but to use the telephone. For some reason he telephoned his sister-in-law Elsie once a week. He could have gone to the Post Office — there was a metal notice outside saying 'You may telephone from here', but by using Father's telephone he stood the chance of having a free call because Father would never bother to ask him for the money. But if it was Mother he saw, he was unlucky, she would stand there with her hand out and say, "That will be tuppence please, Colonel."

Colonel's telephone call went like this:— "Er-er, er-er, — er-er, is that you Else? Uh-huh — uh-huh, — that you Else? Er-er . . . er-er . . . uh-huh, uh-huh, Else, that you Else? Uh-huh, uh-huh, you alright Else? Uh-huh, uh-huh, this is Colonel, Else, uh-huh. Colonel speaking Else — er-er, uh-huh, uh-huh. Can you hear me Else? Uh-huh, oh ah, oh ah, glad you're all right Else, uh-huh, Oh ah, — ah. Just thought I'd give you a tinkle, Else — uh-huh, Else, — uh-huh, I'd better be going, uh-huh Else. Ringing off now Else, oh ah, — oh-ah, well cheerio Else, uh-huh, uh-huh, Goodbye Else."

Colonel was a frequent visitor to Uncle George's too, he went there to drink cider and to talk about pigs — he kept a couple of sows. Since those days as a Lance Corporal in France Colonel had turned his hand to many things, farmwork, forestry, work in the sawmills, and a great variety of odd jobs. He was engaged on odd jobbing and cabbage growing at this time. Last year it had been parsnips — there was going to be a great demand for parsnips last year, the price of parsnips was going sky high. Colonel had planted all his acre with parsnips and he would make a packet out of them. But it turned out that nobody wanted parsnips and Colonel fed as many of them as he could to his pigs (Uncle George said it was like a gasworks down at Colonel's pig styes) and the remainder rotted in the ground.

This year, said Colonel, there was going to be a huge demand for autumn cabbage, an unexpected demand for cabbage, cabbages were going to be priority number one, people would be clamouring for them and he, Colonel, had an acre of them and confidently expected to make a packet, a very pretty little packet indeed.

Chapter 8

A MAN'S A MAN FOR A' THAT

MOST of the farmers had finished haymaking, some hay was stacked in Dutch barns, the rest stood in neat ricks in fields, topped and ready for thatching. Uncle George and I were kept busy in the garden; soon it would be time for the annual fruit, flower and vegetable show. Those vegetables which would shortly be exhibited needed special attention, regular watering, and in the case of the runner beans, thinning out, to ensure that the selected ones could grow to the greatest size possible. We tended them with the utmost care, we cossetted them. Uncle had a reputation to keep up and it would never do to let that Fred Pollard walk off with the prize for beans, not that there was much chance of that.

Runner beans were prized above all other vegetables. The local gardeners were all bean crazy, and it was by the length of your beans you gained kudos. Already a row of them hung from the shelf in The White Lion.

Uncle George had called on most of the competitors, on some pretext or other, and had been able to sneak a look at their vegetables. His report to me was that we hadn't much to worry about, but we must not slacken our efforts. There was always Fred Pollard, and Uncle's dignity would not allow him to be seen snooping about Pollard's garden.

We went and sat on the big upturned flower pots in the honeysuckle-covered garden shed. The shed was in a corner of the garden, and two of its sides were the high walls of the garden. Uncle had made the shed himself; it was large, and a good job that it was too. It housed, besides the large garden pots, the spades, hoes, rakes, dibbers and other garden equipment; several small casks of cider, numerous bottles of home made wines; an oil stove for use on cold winter days. And in one corner hung the seaweed. Uncle foretold the weather by the seaweed. To-day, when he fingered it, it was hard and crisp. "It's going to be dry for some time yet," he said. "We'll have to keep the ooze pipe going to swell the onions and the beetroot, and to keep them byuns a gwain, but mind you," Uncle wrinkled his brow and nose and puffed out his cheeks, "they've got their fit down into that rotten pig muck I dug into the trench last fall." He rubbed the side of his nose with a grimy forefinger and chuckled. He grunted and got to his feet. "C'mon boy, sitting there won't pay the rent, we'll go down into the orchard and have a look at the Perlifics."

The Prolific plums were almost ripe, and the Beauty of Bath apples we looked at would almost certainly take first prize in the Dessert Apple Class. "We'll have to get and cut they 'ettles, boy, or it'll begin to look as wild as old Micah's over there. Damn my rags, ain't that Micah idle. Just look over the hedge there, docks, thistles, 'ettles, and the seed blows over here on my place something cruel. Summat oughta be done about it, but old Micah, he wun't do a durn. Rajah rhubarb, don't that old fish of his stink."

"I can smell smoke, Uncle."

"Ah, I reckon old Amos is having a bonfire. It's Saturday afternoon and he'd be working in his garden. Go and get me the scythe, and a hook for yourself, we'll cut they 'ettles down while we think on't."

As I was returning to the orchard with the scythe and hook, I saw the cause of the smoke, one of Mr. Wilson's hayricks was on fire.

"Uncle, Mr. Wilson's got a hayrick on fire!"

Uncle George looked in the direction I pointed. "Soak me bob, so he has. I told him at the time, that hay was a bit too gay to rick, but he wouldn't hear of it. I told him, there's a lot of fire leaf in that field. 'Pooh,' he said, 'that's all right, that's safe enough, 'tis black and dry.' Now this is the result of not listening to me, he's lost a rick of hay. P'raps next time he'll listen when I give him a bit of advice. He should have kept an eye on that rick and if he'd cut it open when it first got hot he could have saved it. C'mon let's cut these 'ettles down."

We started cutting the nettles and Uncle told me that in the good old days people used to put them to soak and then feed them to pigs. "The 'ettles 'ould go as white as milk."

"Uncle, look! There's another rick afire!" I pointed about a quarter of a mile away from Mr. Wilson's blazing stack.

"Rajah rhubarb! You're right m'boy, proper coincidence that is."

Twenty minutes later we noticed yet another rick on fire. "Dazzed and set it, boy, that ain't no coincidence," said Uncle and wrinkled his brow, "that's them fellas in them airyplanes going over and dropping their fag ends out, that's what that is, I'll warrant."

Fifteen minutes later we saw smoke coming from Mr. Noakes' farm. Uncle hung his scythe in an apple tree, "C'mon boy, let's go and see what the hell fire's up."

We found Mr. Noakes' haybarn was on fire. The fire brigade was just arriving, but Emmanuel Fowler was already recklessly doing his best to fight it alone. The dirty, blackened, hot and sweating figure was hardly recognisable as Emmanuel Fowler, staid Solicitor's Clerk.

"Well, bless my soul," said Uncle George, "just look at that. Who'da thought it of young Manny?"

We stood and watched the Fire Brigade as they pumped water from the lake. Emmanuel continued his work unabated; several times the Fire Chief told him to stand back, to be careful. "You should be in the Brigade, lad," the Fire Chief told him. "We could do with men like you." We stood and watched, and most of the village were there watching by now. Later, something prompted me, I don't know what, to go and see Mr. Wilson's blazing rick.

Late that evening, after most of the excitement had died down, Uncle and I gave the beans a good soaking of water. When we were sitting in the garden shed having a drop of cider, I pulled a handkerchief from my trouser pocket and showed it to Uncle. He looked at it and saw the initials E.F. neatly embroidered in one corner.

"Where did you find this, boy?" he asked.

"Up by Mr. Wilson's rick."

"Have you shown or spoken about it to anybody else?"

"No."

"Um .. um .. um. I always knowed summat like this would happen. Stands to reason — haven't I always said Fowler would break out one day?"

Uncle filled the mug of cider again and lit his pipe and sat silently on the upturned flowerpot, his brow wrinkled, his cheeks puffed. "Keep your mouth shut about this, boy."

I nodded my head and solemnly promised to keep my mouth shut about it.

"Bin a lot of fuss today, boy."

I nodded my head in agreement.

"To my way of thinking, he's been driven to it, like."

"Yes, Uncle."

"Stands to reason, don't it?"

"Yes, Uncle."

"Bin a lot of fires today, boy. One more," he said, putting a match to the handkerchief, "won't hurt."

"No, Uncle."

"Well, just keep mum about it, boy."

But several people said they had seen, or claimed to have seen, somebody like Emmanuel Fowler in the vicinity of the hayricks on that Saturday afternoon and Fowler duly appeared at the local magistrates court.

The Vicar, Mr. Bence, went to give evidence of Fowler's good character, and Fowler conducted his own defence (Mr. Farquharson refused to employ Fowler after he was accused of arson), and did it, said Mr. Bence, brilliantly. The charge was unproven and Fowler was acquitted.

"Lack of evidence, you see," said Uncle George.

Chapter 9

GOSSIP

AT the beginning of August Reuben Kimmins appeared in Court, his second appearance this summer, on a charge of poaching salmon. Reuben was found guilty and was fined.

The Flower Show came, Uncle won .most of the prizes for fruit and vegetables and the local paper had a photograph of him, and me, as Uncle insisted that I, too, should be in the photograph. Fred Pollard scowled and showed off when the prize winners were announced, but the railwaymen who were at the show, cheered and shouted "Good old George."

But apart from Fred Pollard's nastiness, the show day passed off without any untoward incident. "Not like the show day years ago," Uncle George said, "when the policeman got drunk and went and tried to bust up a game of crown and anchor which some strangers were playing at the back of a marquee. The strangers set into him, blacking his eyes and knocking some of his teeth out. Of course, if he'd've bin sober, he'd never have interfered with 'em.

"Why, even the parson got drunk, no, not Mr. Bence, this was afore his time, and was frightened to go home to his missus. 'George, George,' he said to me, 'I can't go home to my wife in this state, I'm quite overcome, I'm not myself, I feel most peculiar.' 'Well,' I said to him, 'I'll give you a bit of a tour round in the sidecar on me motor bike, sir, it will clear your head.' 'A very good idea,' says the vicar, 'it is just what I need in my condition, it will do me the world of good. I just can't understand what's come over me.' No, I thought, I don't suppose you can, you're in a right wassell you are, but it don't take much fathoming out what's the matter with you, you're as drunk as a Lord, as tight as a tick, you old crow, you've had a drop too much to drink, and Heaven help you, if it can, if your old missus sees you like it, she's a real old battleaxe at the best of times and this ain't the best of times for you. Mind, I didn't tell him all that, I just thought it. I bundled him into the sidecar and off we went. He didn't say much, just sang out Hallelujah now and then. Hah, I thought, your missus 'ud Hallelujah you if she saw you now. I drove him round for five or six miles and stopped near the vicarage. 'Feeling better now, sir?' I asked, and he said, 'I think you'd better drive me round again, George, I still feel a little confused.' So, around the course we went again and back near the vicarage I stopped and asked him, 'All right now?' 'Still a little light headed,' he told me. 'I don't think it would be wise to meet my wife in my present state.' Pity you didn't think of that afore you got on the tiddley, I thought, but I said nothing and took him down by the Lake. I pulled up there and had a good mind to chuck him in, that would've sobered him up I'll warrant. 'Drive on, George,' he said, 'somebody might pass by and see us.' Who, I wondered, would be about at that time of night except drunken parsons and silly motor-bike drivers? Anyway, on we went, twenty miles, thirty miles or more we must have driven, this little job was going to cost me a bit in petrol, I was beginning to run a bit low and in any case I'd got fed up with carting him about. There he was, slummocked in the sidecar, he'd given up the Hallelujahs now. I reckon he was getting fair daggled and so I drove back to the village and stopped a little way from the vicarage and heaved him out. I struggled up the vicarage drive with him and got him inside the porch. Then I was flummoxed, what could I do now? I wasn't going to knock on the door and wake his wife up and have her come down and see me. I knew who'd get the blame if she saw me with him. There was a seat fixed to the wall of one side of the porch, so I propped him up there and said to myself, there you stop, you drunken old parson, and may the Lord be with you."

*   *   *

The Show was on Saturday and on Sunday morning Amos Bloxham set about Bonnor Dawes when he delivered the milk. Amos said that on the Thursday morning Bonnor had spent an hour inside the house with his wife. Bonnor often stopped for half an hour or more talking to customers, but Amos was convinced that there was more than talking done on Thursday morning, and knocked Dawes about with a brush handle. Bonnor's face was cut, bruised and swollen and Dr. Higgins had to put four stitches in his chin. Amos was charged with assault and the Court bound him over for twelve months to keep the peace. At home Amos was anything but peaceful, and his wife went to stay at the garage with her brother and his wife until Amos had calmed down.

A few weeks later Bonnor Dawes was in Court again, charged with adding water to his milk. The evidence against him proved insufficient and Bonnor was let off with a caution. But, all in all, during the months of July, August and September our village was well represented at Court.

Talking of Court reminds me that during August we lost our policeman, P.C. Cardew. P.C. Cardew had made no secret of the fact that he did not like his Superintendent and the Superintendent didn't like him. On the night he wrote to the Superintendent, he also wrote to his wife, who was stopping with her sister. Unfortunately, he put the letters in the wrong envelopes, and he has recently been transferred to another part of the County.

The Cricket Team is looking for a new player, and we have a new policeman. The new man is young and keen. 'Out for promotion,' says Arnold Ludgater, who now has to close The Lion sharp on ten o'clock. Already he's had several people for not buying dog licences and Colonel is still wondering if he will have to go to Court on a charge of being drunk and disorderly. Uncle Sam Fisher was fined for riding his bicycle after dark without lights, and is complaining bitterly to all and sundry.

Reuben Kimmins is telling everyone not to worry, "Us'll tame him, never you fear." But Edward Jones doesn't think he is tameable, and is contemplating putting on a regular taxi service from our village to the Court.

* * *

Mr. Pemberthy has extended the ladies' outfitting side of The Emporium. One of his windows is given over to the display of women's clothing. Mother, Mrs. Peabody and Mrs. Gosworth, and others objected strongly to the display of ladies underwear in the window, "Suggestive," they say it is, but they were even more outraged by the model Mr. Pemberthy has bought. He changes the clothes on this model, and is occasionally called away while dressing it. Mother and her friends say it is downright wrong and immoral for Mr. Pemberthy to dress and undress the model in public or private and it is scandalous to let the model remain in the window unclothed.

Mrs. Hatch takes an even firmer line. The sight of the unclothed female model in the window will put lustful thoughts into men's heads and she will certainly not allow Isabel out of the house after dark any more. Everyone, she says, will be raped in their beds. (I heard Uncle George mutter to Reuben, "I don't think some of the old besoms have much to fear, though I reckon it'd do some on 'em good.")

Mrs. Hatch is asking all her customers (which means demanding) to sign petitions about it, one to send to the Bishop, the other to her M.P. Meanwhile, Mr. Pemberthy is not allowed a daily paper.

Even Uncle George admits he can never remember the village in such a buzz of gossip. Miss Zebrina Ellicot, the pretty young daughter of Mr. Trophimus Ellicot, has run off with a young man who was stopping at The Rose and Crown. Mrs. Hatch, who sees the blackest side of everything, calls it kidnapping, and will not allow Isabel out in the daytime now unless accompanied. Uncle George says there is absolutely no fear of Isabel being kidnapped in daylight.

* * *

The summer holidays over, we are back at school and Mrs. Simpkins is no better. She has now taken to lecturing us on world affairs. The Prime Minister has just returned from Munich and Mrs. Simpkins, with tears in her eyes tells us, "Mr. Chamberlain has saved us all, dear Mr. Chamberlain is a British hero."

Mr. Teakle takes a different view. When I took a pair of shoes into his shop for repair. Mr. Teakle was unaccustomedly grave. "Never," he said, "did I think I'd stand in this shop and say I'm ashamed of being English, yet, to-day I am deeply ashamed. We have betrayed our friends in Europe, one after another. We have broken our promises, it is one long terrible disgrace, and one day we shall pay dearly for it. It should never have happened, and would not have happened if Mr. Lloyd George had been a younger man and still Prime Minister. I do not like war, I went through the last one and was gassed, I know the horror of war, but there comes a time, and it came a long time ago, when an honourable man must say halt, and, if need be, take up arms against the oppressor. War is bound to come, thanks to that old apple woman Chamberlain and his clique of quivering yes-men."

"But Mrs. Simpkins says Mr. Chamberlain has saved us all and is a hero," I said.

"Poppycock!" said Mr. Teakle. "That woman is a fool and it's her sort who have put fools into power. If Chamberlain and that Baldwin had acted honourably years ago war could have been averted. Now, it's inevitable."

* * *

Mr. Teakle was quite right about Mrs. Simpkins. She is a fool, and a fortnight after Mr. Teakle's conversation I began to think she had gone right off her head.

It all began after the afternoon playtime. Every afternoon playtime we gathered at the school railings to see old Mr. Brimble

returning from The Lion. If he was drunk he would stop to dance a jig and sing for us in the road. We watched him dance with horrible fascination. Rumour had it that he had been injured in such a way in the Great War that he had to have a bottle strapped between his legs. We reasoned, since he'd spent all morning in The Lion, the bottle would be full and that one day while he was dancing it would go crashing to the ground.

When we were back in the classroom we saw Mrs. Simpkins had the nasty turkey look, and sure enough she soon turned vicious. Ronald is called out in front and she starts rapping his knuckles for all she's worth. I think her brain must have snapped because she goes on rapping mercilessly, her face becoming redder and redder. Ronald's face was white, he'd had more than enough, and who could blame him when he ground his nailed boot into her soft glossy leather shoe?

"Ooh! ooh! ooh!" she screamed. Of course, she's mad, you know. "Ooh! ooh! ooh!" and starts to jump about like billy-ho. I felt like laughing, but dared not, you never know what mad women will do. "Miss Lockit, Miss Lockit, quick, quick." Old Locky rushes in from the infants room like a pekinese after a mouse, her black, beady eyes looking as if they'd pop right out — of course she's mad too. They should both be put away, but, as I learnt from a Sexton Blake story, mad people are very often cunning, and these two certainly

64

are, they can always contrive to appear almost normal in front of grown ups. But when it's only school children they don't half let rip. Coo, I wish the Inspector or Mr. Bence would walk in when they were having a turn, they'd soon see then what the pair of them are really like.

"Get the cane, Miss Lockit," screamed Simpky. "Get the cane, and the black book." Mad as a hatter she was and ferocious with it, but Ronald wasn't going to stand there for her to go berserk with the cane, and I didn't blame him either. "Stop him! stop him!" screamed Simpky, frothing at the mouth; and both of them leapt at him.

Round and round the room the three of them went, desks, pens, pencils, books and inkwells went flying. Poor old Ronald struggled on, Simpky and Locky pulling and tugging, clawing and spitting and squawking. The rest of us just looked on, frightened and speechless. One or two of the girls started crying, another screamed. The infants heard the noise and some of them started caterwauling — oh, it really was dreadful. Eventually they got Ronald caught in a corner and overcame him, but he'd put up a good struggle. They say mad people have double strength, so really he'd done very well indeed. The three of them stopped in the corner for some time, puffing and panting and then Simpky said, "We'll put him in the infants' room, Miss Lockit." They pushed him into the infants room and brought all the infants into our room, the poor little devils were frightened to death, and no wonder, so were we. No doubt Simpky and Locky thought in their demented minds that Ronald had some infectious disease and everyone would catch it if he wasn't isolated.

Mrs. Simpkins kept saying that she wouldn't have Ronald at the school another day, and she would write to the Education Committee; and Miss Lockit kept on going to have a squint at poor old Ronald.

Ronald was back at school on Monday, and nothing's been said about it since. I suppose Simpky and Locky are partially sane now, but we are going very careful, the slightest thing may unbalance them and you never know what mad people may do.

* * *

The next Saturday I told Uncle George and Reuben about them while we were picking up the cider apples. Colonel was there too and he said, "They need a couple of big rough men round them." It would need some big rough men to deal with them too when their brains snap.

Uncle had to stop picking up apples because he had 'a touch of the screws come on' and so he sat on a fruit box and watched us. He kept reciting the names of cider apples,

> "Coccagee and Bloody Butcher,
> Slack-ma-Girdle,
> Red Soldier and Lady's Finger,
> Kingston Black, Bloody Turk,
> Fox Whelp, Pawson, Tom Putt,
> Bitter Sweet and Fatty Mutt."

His deep, rich fruity voice made them sound like poetry.

We were working up by Micah Elford's garden and after a while Micah poked his head over the hedge and said, "You bin quatting on that box some time, George."

"And what odds is that to you, Micah?" Uncle George asked.

"Oh, it's like that, is it?" said Micah and went away.

"Nosey old varmint" said Uncle George. "I'm glad he's gone," and recited his list of apples again.

"Well," he said, about five minutes later. "You ain't tamed the Bobby yet, Reuben. I see he copped you a poaching pheasants."

"No, I think he's untameable; he's a wrong 'un you know," replied Reuben.

"How d'you get on at Court?" asked Uncle.

"Oh, they fined I five pun, and the chairman said, 'Kimmins, this is the third time this year you've been up before me for poaching, the next time it'll be prison.' And then he tells I, quite friendly like, 'but I will say this for you, Kimmins, you never poach game out of season'."

"Hark! hark!" said Uncle, holding up his hand, "Hark at that old Micah and his missus having a set-to."

We stopped work and listened.

"I'm sick and tired of that disgusting old thing down the garden," said Mrs. Elford. "Why can't we have a decent one in the house?"

"No drains," answered Micah.

"Why can't we have one of those chemical ones, then, in the garden? They've got some at the hardware store."

"There's nothing the matter with what we've got, and why spend money on them chemical contraptions?" asked Micah.

"It wouldn't cost much to nail the boards up at the back for a start."

"Them holes do let the air in and keep it sweet."

"It isn't very sweet in there, and it isn't decent either with them holes at the back."

"Her's right you know," said Uncle George quietly. "Old Micah's as mean as the devil and that old privy of their'n do stink something roaring — still, what can you expect from a man who eats a lot of stinking old fish?"

66

We went on picking up apples and after a door slammed over the other side of the hedge Uncle George said, "There's old Micah gone into his privy now, to get rid of another load of stinking old fish — hark! hark! can you hear the old varmint a grunting?"

"Aaaaaaaah . . . aaaaaaah . . ." came a terrible yell.
"Good God, whatever's that?" asked Reuben.
"Summat's up," said Colonel.
"I'd aim the old varmint's exploded," said Uncle George.
After a few minutes Mrs. Elford looked over the hedge and asked, "Did you hear him holler? I've been on at him to repair the back of that privy, but he wouldn't, so I waited my chance and when he was sat in there just now I pushed a bunch of stinging nettles through, and gave his behind a fair tickling. He didn't half rear up, and I'm off out for a bit now to give his behind a chance to cool down."
"Serve the old bugger right," said Uncle George after she'd gone. "That woman's too good for the likes of him. I wonder how she put up with him and his stinking old fish."
The following Saturday, Uncle George was cider making, with the help of Colonel and Reuben. The apples were crushed with a machine driven by a petrol engine, and the pomace then placed in layers between cider mats on the press. One of Uncle's Old Spot Sows strolled up to the heap of apples outside the cider house, and after eating a few mouthfuls of the apples, crouched over the heap, arching her back and lifting her tail. "Look," said Uncle, "at that old sow a pissing over them apples. Drive her off, Colonel."
"Make the cider stronger," said Colonel.
"Well, I don't want that in my cider," said Uncle. "Go and shut her up in the cot."

"Mind," said Reuben, as Colonel drove the pig away, "cider'll purify anything."

"Oha, and yut anything," said Uncle. "I remember when they used to make a lot of cider at Noakes', not this young Noakes, nor his father, but his grandfather, great vats of it they made and sold. One year they had a hoss die, and they put a whole leg of the hoss in a vat of this cider and do you know that when they came to clean out the vat the next year, there weren't a morsel of that great leg to be seen, the cider had yut every bit on it."

Uncle paused for a moment and then said, "If you give cider something to yut, it makes it stronger, a lot stronger — but that don't mean as I wants a lot of droppings and suchlike in my cider. Colonel, the old fool, ought to have more sense than to have let the sow do a trick like that." He smiled at us, and said in an undertone, "I hear there's a lot of cabbage going to waste up at his place, I ought to be able to buy some cheap for my pigs."

* * *

The day we broke up for the Christmas holidays, Mrs. Simpkins and Miss Lockit made an effort, I grant them that, to appear sane and affable. Mind you, it was a bit of a strain for them, you could see that. They gave us an orange each and then Mrs. Simpkins gave us a talk about Christmas. "Christmas," she said, "is Jesus' birthday. I hope you'll all go to Church on His birthday to Worship Him and to praise Him. If you don't go, it won't be very kind, having celebrations at home and forgetting all about Him on His birthday. How would you like to be shut up in an attic on your birthday while people had a party downstairs? If you don't go to Church on Christmas Day, you'll be shutting Jesus up in an attic on His birthday and making Him sad on His birthday. As I've told you, over and over again, you must be kind to everyone, especially on their birthdays."

"Please Mrs., you caned me on my birthday," said Ronald. Old Simpky pretended she hadn't heard him, but she heard all right.

"Hands up now, all who promise to go to Church on Jesus' birthday," she said quickly. We put our hands up to please her and shut her up, all except Tom.

"Tom," she said, "I didn't see your hand up."

"I didn't put it up, Mrs. Simpkins," said Tom.

"Why not? Why won't you promise to go to Church on Jesus' birthday? Jesus will be upset if you don't go and God will be angry with you."

"Please, my dad don't believe in God," answered Tom.

"Oh dear, oh dear, oh dear, poor Tom. Poor Tom's father,

children, he will go to a bad place if he doesn't believe in God, children. Before you go home, let's all kneel down and pray for Tom's father to believe."

She made us all kneel down and pray to God to make Tom's father believe in God. Old Simpky's potty, but we have to humour her.

Mr. Bence, the choir and a few more of us went round singing carols and collecting for charity just before Christmas, and Colonel, who's always drunk just before Christmas, wrote out his usual cheque for £10. Mr. Bence thanked him very much, but I knew that he tore it up later, because he knew that it was unlikely that Colonel would have more than a pound in the bank and if there were more, Mrs. Biggs needed it.

They were as poor as could be, the cabbages had let Colonel down as badly as the parsnips had the year before. Not that Colonel was despondent, already he was saying there'd be a big demand for lettuce next summer.

* * *

Soon after Christmas, Mr. Pontifex was seriously ill and taken to hospital. We all thought he was going to die, but after a month in hospital he was well enough to go to a convalescent home. When he had recovered he became restive and pleaded to be allowed to return to his home. Dr. Higgins said he would not allow him to go home until he agreed to have someone to live with him and look after him. No, no, Mr. Pontifex wouldn't agree, but at last he gave way. I think it was the thoughts of his piano and music that did it. He sent a note to Gert asking would she please come and be his housekeeper, and she agreed.

So now we can hear the sound of Mr. Pontifex's piano again, and some evenings it isn't only classical music we hear, but musical comedy tunes and the sound of Gert's singing. That isn't all either; Mr. Pontifex, Gert and the house are all transformed, all remarkably clean and tidy.

Of course, there's been a lot of talk by some people in the village about Mr. Pontifex and Gert. Mrs. Hatch in particular was very nasty about it, but there was nothing she could do. Mr. Pontifex had never bothered to have a paper, so she couldn't even be spiteful in that way. And neither Mr. Pontifex nor Gert had ever cared two hoots what people said about them.

Mother didn't approve, and said to Mr. Teakle, "Dirty he might have been, but I always thought he was a gentleman, but he can't be, having that woman living with him."

"Ma'am" replied Mr. Teakle, "gentlemen, like ladies, come in all sorts of guises and classes, and I feel honoured to be able to call Mr. Pontifex and Gert friends of mine and will not allow anybody to speak ill of them in my presence."

"Oh!" said Mother and looked abashed.

"I'm sorry ma'am," said Mr. Teakle, "I did not wish to appear rude, but I've heard so much ill-natured talk about those two, and I'm so happy that they're so happy, that I'm liable to speak a little sharply if I hear anyone criticise them. If I was rude, I do hope you'll accept my humble apologies."

"Well," said Mother, when we'd left the shop, "I just don't know what to make of Mr. Teakle."

Chapter 10

IN WHICH OUR VILLAGE HAS A MEETING, AND WE HAVE A VISITOR

"IT'S the Parish Meeting tonight, boy," said Uncle George. "You and I, we'll go along and hear what's said, and maybe say a word or two ourselves, if the need do arise."

When we arrived at the hall, there was quite a crowd there. "Oho", said Uncle George, "there's a fair few here; summat's in the wind you may depend. Usually, very few bother to turn up, but from what I can see of some on 'em here tonight, 'tis more'n likely there'll be a barney afore the night's out."

We sat in the front row in a couple of rickety old chairs. "They wants to get some new chairs for a start," observed Uncle George.

I turned round and looked about. Mrs. Peabody, Mrs. Gosworth, and Mrs. Gerrish were sitting together in the centre of the hall. Uncle Sam Fisher was just behind us. He took a large handkerchief out of his pocket and blew his nose loudly. His big moustache waggled. He blew for a long time and when he'd finished, he looked hard at his handkerchief to see what he'd blown. He always did that; Father called it a disgusting habit.

Mrs. Hatch was sitting in the front row at the far end from us, and so was Mr. Elford. At the back, in a corner, sat Amos Bloxham, buttoned up in an old army greatcoat. Reuben came and sat down beside us. Mrs. Lloyd sat at one side of the hall, Mrs. Heckitt at the other. Several more people were sitting closely together at the back, I couldn't see who they all were, but I just managed to get a glimpse of Mr. Paget, the postman, Fred Jenkins, cowman at Carter's farm, and Ronald Ferneyhough.

In front and facing us was the Parish Council, Mr. Winkleberry the Chairman (the Mayor) in the centre and Mr. Bingle, the clerk, next to him. Mr. Tucker, Mr. Noakes, Mr. Wilson, Mr. Gosworth, Mr. Gerrish and Mr. Dawes, all councillors, were sitting up there. They all looked self-important, but a little embarrassed.

Mr. Teakle came and sat by me, and the Vicar sat next to him. "Oho," said Uncle George, "quite a gathering. There's old Mother Hatch over there. I'll bet she's come to cause a rumpus, and old Mothers Lloyd and Heckitt'll have a quarrel, that's for certain."

While Mr. Winkleberry was welcoming everyone and saying how pleased he was that so many people had come, but looking as if he'd have been better pleased if they hadn't, Fred Pollard came in and sat down in the chair behind Uncle.

The Clerk, Mr. Bingle, a prissy man who earned his living as an insurance agent, and lived in an ugly little red brick house like a box, called The Villa, outside the village, read the minutes of the last annual Parish Meeting. The minutes were signed, and a brief discussion followed. Then Mr. Winkleberry gave a fulsome speech, outlining the previous year's activities of the Council. They didn't sound very impressive.

Up jumps Fred Pollard. "That's as maybe, but what about the holes in the High Street? What about the blocked footpaths and the broken footbridges, eh? What about the smells, the flooding of the roads? What about all the rats on the rubbish tip? What do you Councillors do? I'll tell you what you do, damn all but sit on your arses and talk." While he was speaking Pollard gripped the back of Uncle's chair, pushing it back and forth.

"If you don't shut up, and stop waggling my chair, Fred Pollard, I'll kick thy great fat arse," said Uncle George.

"Oooh, such language!" said Mrs. Hatch.

"There's ladies present," said the Clerk.

Micah Elford lumbers to his feet. "And what are you doing about the smell of pigs, which is ruining my property?" he asked.

Uncle was on his feet in a flash. "There's a terrible smell of stinking old fish about his place," he said.

"Gentlemen, gentlemen," pleaded Mr. Winkleberry and flapped his hands.

"What do we pay rates for?" asked Fred Pollard.

"Ah now, there's a question, what do we pay rates for?" asked Micah Elford.

"We ain't got no street lights," said Pollard.

"Now, now, gentlemen be reasonable, we haven't any gas or electricity," pleaded Mr. Winkleberry and fussed with some papers.

"And why haven't we got 'em?" asked Davie Bridges, signalman. "I'll tell 'ee for why, 'cos they'm in private hands, they should be nationalised, that's what."

"We want a Labour Government," said Eddy Bridges, railway ganger and brother of Davie.

"Bolsheviks!" shrieked Mrs. Hatch. "We're riddled with Bolsheviks."

"Yer nothing but a bunch of old Tories on the Council," said Davie Bridges.

"Bolsheviks! That's what you two are, Bolsheviks!" Mrs. Hatch was beside herself. "I always knew it and my Ebenezer always has said that railwaymen are Reds."

"Please, please," said Mr. Winkleberry, "no politics, if you please."

"And why not?" demanded Eddy Bridges.

"Because, we don't have politics on the Parish Council," said Mr. Winkleberry.

"Oh you don't, don't yer. As long as you're all Tories on there, there ain't no politics. If 'twere Labour men you'd say 'twas all bloody politics" said Eddy Bridges.

"He's got a point there, Mr. Chairman," said Mr. Teakle and, in an aside to me, "I really think that at long last our parish may be getting politically conscious and vocal."

"I will not have this bad language," said Mr. Winkleberry.

"I quite agree, Mr. Mayor, I should bloody well think not," said Uncle George.

Mr. Winkleberry was about to say something, but was interrupted by Mrs. Lloyd who shouted, "He's quite right, we want electricity."

Mrs. Heckitt waved her brolly and shouted, "We need water, we need water."

"Order! Order!" said Mr. Winkleberry.

"Electricity," shouted Mrs. Lloyd.

"Water," shouted Mrs. Heckitt.

"Order," shouted Mr. Winkleberry.

"Electricity," "Water," "Order, order."

"Shut up and let the Mayor speak," shouted Uncle.

"If you don't behave in a more orderly fashion, I shall close the meeting," said Mr. Winkleberry.

After this, the meeting was conducted in a more orderly fashion, and several more topics were discussed. A great many problems would, said the Chairman, have to lie on the table. Uncle George muttered that there couldn't be room left on the table for much more. The council would, said Mr. Winkleberry, be busy discussing air raid precautions in the coming months. Soon afterwards the meeting closed.

* * *

At Easter, Uncle George, Father and I went once again to see the Severn Bore. We did not know it at the time, but this would be the last time the three of us would go together to see the bore. This time we went higher up stream where the river was narrower and there was quite a crowd standing near the river bank when we arrived. The Bore was disappointing, hardly more than a foot high.

"Poorish old Bore," said Uncle George, as we drove along the road to The Sloop, where the beer was first class.

"Last time we came along here there was mud on the road, where the tide had come over," said Father.

"The road were slick."

"Ah, it were that, George."

"Devilish slick."

"You managed all right though, didn't you, George?"

"A man had his taters up."

"And you said the frost would cut 'em off."

"That's right, I did."

"And we bought some elvers at The Sloop, George."

This year there were no elvers for sale at The Sloop, but about half a mile further along the road, we met a woman and a boy on bicycles who had elvers for sale.

"It's the first year me son's caught elvers and he's a bit shy selling 'em on his own, so I'm going with him. He'll be all right next year," said the woman.

"Did he have a good catch?" asked Uncle George.

"Very good, Sir. Beginner's luck I told him."

"We'll have four pints apiece then," said Father.

"Be a bit of pocket money for him," I said, "and he'll be able to buy hisself a pair of new shoes."

"I'll give him an extra shilling, as this is his first year," said Uncle George.

"That's very kind of you, Sir. You want to boil 'em and put 'em in a pudden basin and when they're cold they turn out just like a jelly — you'll like 'em like that," she said.

As we drove home Uncle George said, "I shouldn't want elvers cold."

"No more would I. I'd rather have 'em fried with a nice bit of your fat bacon, George."

"So would I, or done in egg and breadcrumbs."

"You're supposed to have fish on a Good Friday," said Father.

"Shouldn't want any of Micah's stinking old fish though, nor any of Banstead's hot cross buns, they didn't half give me the heartburn last year," said Uncle George.

"Ethel won't buy any off him, says she couldn't fancy them, with him living with those two women."

"Man's a damned fool."

"Daresay you're right, George."

"Pemberthy's going in for men's ready-made suits now," said Uncle George.

"Ah, I've seen 'em. Not much cop, light as a feather."

"The man's a keen business man."

"He's a fly one, George, that's what he is."

"Don't like the look of the news."

"There's going to be a war I'm afraid, George," said Father.

*　　*　　*

In June we had a visitor. Aunt Dorothea arrived by train and Mother and I went in Mr. Jones' car to the station to meet her. On the way home I saw Uncle George coming out of The Lion. Mother was looking straight ahead. "Isn't that your brother-in-law coming out of that public house?" asked Aunt Dorothea.

"I didn't see him," said Mother.

"But you must have done." Aunt Dorothea spoke with a curious brittle voice — cracking her jaw, Father called it.

"No, I didn't, but it wouldn't surprise me."

"He drinks too much, Ethel. I shouldn't let this young man spend too much time with him."

That evening Uncle George called and said, "Hullo Dotty, how are you?"

"I'm very well, thank you, but I've told you before, my name is Dorothea."

"You allus was Dotty and you allus will be Dotty as far as I'm concerned," replied Uncle George.

After he'd gone Aunt Dorothea told Mother, "I never liked that man, coarse, idle good for nothing."

"You don't know what I've got to put up with, Dorothea, he's the plague of my life."

"I should stop him coming here, Ethel."

"I would, but Father's that overseen in him."

"You should put your foot down, Ethel, I wouldn't allow my Egbert to bring riff-raff to my home, not that my Egbert ever would."

"I show him that he's not wanted, but he's that hardened."

"And that rapscallion Kimmins he's so friendly with. When we were girls we did not associate with the likes of the Kimmins'. Guttersnipes, our parents called that brood of Kimmins'. Keep yourself to yourself, we were taught. Why! the man's a criminal, I read all about him in the papers you sent, Ethel. Kimmins is nothing less than a common thief. Then there's that man Biggs — Colonel indeed! He's a drunken wastrel. That's the kind of low-bred men your brother-in-law associates with — birds of a feather, I always say. Thank goodness I married into a respectable family, not that I would have dreamt of marrying into anything else of course, nobody can say I wasn't sensible — yes, and though I say it myself — refined. It's been such a help to Egbert to have a wife who is ladylike. The Bank is very particular about the wives of their staff you know. Gracious! If they knew I was in any way, however remote, connected with such a disreputable character as that George, it would do poor Egbert's career irreparable damage."

You silly swanking, stuck-up old cat, I thought, you're as potty as old Simpky.

But the thing that really got her going was the old tin tray performance. Apparently she was walking up the High Street when Uncle George came bounding along, walloping the tray and hollering, hotly followed by a bevy of yapping dogs and delighted children. Uncle George seemed amused rather than embarrassed by his noisy followers. When he sighted Aunt Dorothea he bellowed, "A swarm of bees in June is worth a silver spoon — you were born with one in your mouth, Dotty, but, as you can see, I've got to chase mine," and with that rushed off banging and shouting "Tally-ho! Tally-ho!".

That evening he called to see Father and greeted Aunt Dorothea, "I lost my silver spoon this afternoon, Dotty, but from the looks on your face, I should say you've swallowed yourn."

"The trouble with you, George, is that you don't take life seriously — you treat it as a joke," said Aunt Dorothea.

"If I took life seriously, Dotty, I couldn't bear it," answered Uncle George.

"I don't call your insulting behaviour a joke," replied my Aunt.

"Make up your mind, Dotty, first you say it's a joke, then you say it ain't; you can't be of the same mind for two seconds." He paused and wrinkled his nose. "I say, Ethel, have you got a bit of bi-carbonate of soda, I seem to have run right out of it and my chase this afternoon has given me a spot of indigestion, unless 'twas the bread pudding I had for tea," said Uncle George and belched.

"Ooh!" gasped Aunt Dorothea. "Have you no manners? Never, not in all the years I've been married to Egbert, have I ever heard him make a disgusting noise like that."

Mother and I saw Aunt Dorothea off on the train, and as she poked her head out of the window to wave goodbye, Mother said, "If the war comes, Dorothea, you had better come and stay with us." And Aunt Dorothea replied, "Thank you very much Ethel, but I'd rather face the bombs than that George, day after day."

Chapter 11

THE SHELTER AND A SPY SCARE

THE war came, as Mr. Teakle had predicted it would. Caspar Rochester departed for an unknown destination. Old Mr. Palmer camouflaged his white gate by daubing it with blobs of brown, black and green paint. Some evacuees arrived and were billeted around the parish.

Edward Jones' son Bert, that chaser of 'hot arsed wenches,' joined the army and Mr. Jones said, "I don't know how I'll manage without our Bert, he was such a good boy for work, never thought of anything but work, work, work."

Uncle Sam Fisher became an air raid warden. He spent a lot of his time cycling slowly up and down the village, wearing a tin hat and a look of solemn authority. Often he would give rasping blasts on his whistle, but later this was replaced by a loud hailer through which he bellowed, "Air raid! Air raid! Take cover."

"Who orthodoxed that Sam Fisher to keep having air raids?" Uncle George asked belligerently. Even Mr. Bence was heard to remark, "I admire his keenness, but I do wish Warden Fisher would ration his practice raids to only one or two a month."

A mild little German Jew and his daughter, who had been living in the village since they escaped from Hitler two years ago, were interned. Mrs. Hatch loudly proclaimed that Davie and Eddy Bridges and other Bolsheviks should also be interned.

The farmers started ploughing some of their pastures. A large house a mile away from the village, which had been empty for some years, was converted into a hostel to accommodate Land Girls.

*　　*　　*

And Uncle George built an Air Raid Shelter in his garden.

While digging the pit, Uncle was overcome 'by a touch of the screws.' Reuben Kimmins was called in to help. Colonel was coming too, but decided he'd better take advantage of the fine weather and plough his lettuce in. Next year he planned to grow potatoes — potatoes were always in great demand in wartime. "That," said Colonel, "is something I do know; I spent most of the last war peeling spuds — the army exists on spuds and plum jam."

Old railway sleepers, wooden stakes and rusty corrugated iron were used to build the shelter. Uncle George sat on an upturned fruit

box, a bottle of cider at his side, and gave instructions to Reuben. Occasionally, he would lumber to his feet and show Reuben where to drive a stake in and then return to his box to, as he put it, survey the construction. He'd give instructions for a stake or a post to be moved slightly and bellow, "Not that 'un, thick 'un!" or "Move thic 'un to the right — ah — ah — ah — to the left now." "Dammit all, George, that's where I had the bugger in the fust place," said a flustered Reuben. "Chun't, Reuben, and you do know darn well chun't." When the shelter was finished, it resembled his garden shed, except that half of it was below ground and the rusty corrugated iron roof was covered with turves instead of honeysuckle.

Uncle George went round the village inviting everyone to come and view his shelter. Even Mother was prevailed upon and when she saw it she said, "It's not very substantial George. I wouldn't risk my neck going into it even when there were no bombs about."

I didn't think Father was very nice about it, either, when he said, "It'll make a nice tatey house, George, but it 'ouldn't stop a firework." And later I heard him say to Mother, "Our George seems to be going a bit childish."

But Uncle and I were immensely proud of his shelter and we'd sit in the garden shed and admire it. "We'll get a barrel of cider down in there Sunday morning, boy. I can't understand why your Father don't build one down at his place; I have offered to come and help him. Now you just remember, boy if you hear the sirens go, you rush up here as hard as you can, if everyone else wants to be blown to smithereens it ain't my fault."

* * *

More young men went from the village into the army. Wheat was planted in the newly ploughed fields. Most of the evacuees returned home, but the two who had been billeted on Mr. Pontifex and Gert remained. Both Mr. Pontifex and Gert made a great fuss of their young charges. "God," murmured Mr. Bence to Uncle George and me as Gert passed us in the High Street, with a look of serene content on her face and a smiling child clutching each hand, "moves in mysterious ways."

Uncle and I were just going into the Newsagents and saw a picture of a broadly smiling soldier saying goodbye to his wife and young daughter on the cover of *Illustrated*. Uncle George studied the picture with a frown upon his face and muttered, "Ah, and I wonder how he do really feel."

* * *

Much to everyone's relief Sam Fisher had gone to work in a munitions factory — at least we shouldn't have to endure his air raids between the hours of eight and six. Aunt Aggie was prouder of her Sam than ever. "My Sam is engaged on essential war work. It is what they call hush-hush work and very secret. My Sam is a key-worker and more than that I dare not tell you."

The Land Girls came, and filled the tap room of The White Lion every Saturday night. Mother and her friends called them brazen young hussies, drinking in public bars, and their faces and lips gay with rouge and lipstick. Their hands, however, were blistered and chapped, their fingernails broken. "They must find the work arduous," said Mr. Teakle, "yet they are so willing and cheerful — these are some of the real English, part of the England I am proud of."

* * *

The winter and the rain came too, and poor Uncle George's shelter was flooded. Mother wasn't slow to point out to him that his shelter wasn't even any good for storing potatoes. Uncle George was despondent until something happened to make him – and me – forget all about the shelter.

Since Uncle George had become a full time smallholder, he'd taken to going to market every week to "study the pig trade." And, Mother said, "to drink whisky, by the smell of him." On return he'd feed his pigs and then come to see Father to tell him about the state of the market. Often he had some news of a doctor at the hospital, "I heard to-day that old Berry is retiring, they'll have a job to replace him, devilish clever chap at diagnosing. They do say that there was nobody in Harley Street to equal him."

Sometimes he'd tell us about some wonderful new remedy he'd purchased in town, "I only read about it yesterday in the *News of the World*. By all accounts it's absolutely A.1." After rummaging in his pockets he'd produce the newspaper cutting, "Here it is, all in black and white, just the very stuff for my trouble. I bought a dozen packets of it while I was in town, there's bound to be a rush on it."

After supper Uncle George and Father would settle down to discuss more of the *News of the World* scandals. "Some devilish bad baggers about, George", my father would say, and Uncle would nod his head and solemnly agree.

One market day, in early December, Uncle George came round much earlier than usual; he was in a state of excitement.

"Do you know they've caught a spy in town?" he said. "Had his equipment down in a cellar under a chemist's shop – if they hadn't caught him, I reckon he'd have poisoned the lot of us." He paused and blew his cheeks out and looked very grave. "It's my opinion the place is swarming with 'em."

After that spies became an obsession with Uncle George and me. It may have been a coincidence, but Sexton Blake was very busy at that time battling with spies. We spent hours in the garden shed discussing the problem. "Can't understand your father. Here we are with spies all round us, they're infested with 'em in town and he won't even listen to me when I tell him. I saw a couple of chaps in town the other day and I could have sworn they were spies. When you've read as much about spies as I have you can have a pretty shrewd idea. It's my opinion the country is alive with 'em, can't understand why the government don't do something about it, bunch of duffers I call 'em." Uncle George filled the cup with cider and stared in gloomy silence, his brow lined and his cheeks puffed out. After a time he exclaimed, "Rajah rhubarb! If we filled in the bottom of that shelter, 'twould make a tidy little farrowing house."

Uncle George began to write letters to the Home Secretary accusing local people of being spies. The letters were followed by visits from the policeman. Uncle George began to get quite angry. "I had another visit from that Bobby, the Home Secretary must have told him about my letter again, though I marked it Highly Confidential — fellow must be an absolute duffer — he should get in touch with me direct. Anyway, I sent that fool of a policeman off with a flea in his ear. I told him that I wouldn't need to write to the Home Secretary if he did his job properly instead of wasting his time pestering me because he saw me out round my farrowing sows at night with a lantern." Uncle George was fuming about the inadequacies of the government, the secret service and the police when the Vicar called and asked him to organise, and give talks to, the Pig Club and the Dig for Victory campaign. "You couldn't have come to a better man, Vicar," said Uncle, and he was soon so busy and engrossed in these new interests that he almost forgot about the spies.

Uncle George put his heart and soul into the pig and gardening efforts. At one time I thought he was spending too much time at it and I told him so. "Well then, boy," he replied, "you'd better come along and give me a hand. Apart from meself there ain't a fellow in the parish who knows as much about pigs and gardening as you do." Uncle George gave lengthy and detailed talks in the village hall and I would sit among the audience feeling very proud when he spoke about gardening, pigs, poultry and orchards.

Chapter 12

PARISH DEFENCE BRIGADE

IT began to snow in late December, and we had the coldest, hardest winter for years. The Severn froze and a local paper had pictures of a policeman cycling on the frozen river. Father made a toboggan and Tom and I spent happy hours riding down the steep bank of Farmer Noakes' big field. Pig food became scarce and Uncle George had to exercise all his ingenuity to obtain enough to feed his pigs. Eventually he had to sell some of them and he called the Minister of Agriculture a blundering fool.

Newspapers became smaller and in short supply, some magazines ceased publication (including the *Sexton Blake Weekly*, though the monthly *Sexton Blake Library* series still continued). Mrs. Hatch became more autocratic, and when the young man who delivered her papers was called up, she said, "If you want a daily paper you fetch it, or go without."

One Saturday morning Mr. Teakle was collecting his *News Chronicle* when I called for Father's *Daily Mail*. She was in the middle of a tirade about the Bridges brothers. "Bolsheviks, the two of them — they should be in the army or interned. They are now saying, if you please, that we should have a government of the people. Of the people indeed! They mean a Bolshevik government, that's what they mean! Revolution! Violence! Bloodshed! They'd have us murdered in our beds! They should be locked up!"

"Come, come, Mrs. Hatch. Eddy and Davie aren't Bolsheviks, nor lovers of violence, neither of them would wilfully harm any innocent person and you know it," said Mr. Teakle.

"In this very shop! I tell you, in this very shop, they said it! A government of the real people of England, they said."

"Ah, I agree with them there, it's time we got rid of the guilty men. Look," said Mr. Teakle and pointed to two posters stuck on the wall opposite the shop, "at those posters. That's what they say and that's what they mean and yet they're too stupid to see what's wrong with it."

I read the official posters, and so did Mrs. Hatch. In vivid red with white lettering:

FREEDOM IS IN PERIL

　　　DEFEND IT WITH ALL YOUR MIGHT

　　　and on the second one:

　　　YOUR COURAGE

　　　YOUR CHEERFULNESS

　　　YOUR RESOLUTION

　　　WILL BRING US

　　　VICTORY.

"I can't see anything wrong with that," snapped Mrs. Hatch.

"Perhaps you can't," said Mr. Teakle quietly. "Perhaps you can't, Mrs. Hatch, but I can and so can Davie and Eddy."

"Really, Mr. Teakle, really I'm surprised at you, siding with those two, and to think I always thought the *News Chronicle* was a respectable paper," said a puzzled Mrs. Hatch.

People were singing 'We're Gonna Hang Out The Washing On the Siegfried Line', and George Formby sang 'Imagine Me In The Maginot Line'.

The newspapers called it the Bore War, but Mr. Teakle called it the lull before the storm.

Mr. Churchill made a speech, "Come then; let us to the task, to the battle, to the toil ... Fill the armies, rule the air, pour out the munitions ... not a week, nor a day, nor an hour to lose."

"In that case", asked Mr. Teakle, "why are there still over a million unemployed?" People like Father, Gosworth, Pemberthy, shook their heads. It wasn't only Mrs. Hatch who didn't understand Mr. Teakle.

* * *

But to Tom and me, tobogganing in that crisp snow in Mr. Noakes' steep field, the war seemed very remote and we were scarcely touched by it. Even the rationing which people complained about was of small concern to us, and Mr. Teakle's cryptic remarks meant little or nothing.

Then Uncle George began to talk about the possibilities of an invasion in the spring. He, like Mr. Teakle, was very disgruntled by the conduct of the government. "This poor old country of ours is at the mercy of a bunch of nogmen," he grumbled.

We saw little of Reuben or Colonel. The War Ag (War Agricultural Executive Committee), had declared war on the rabbits which threatened to destroy the newly planted corn and Reuben was employed to shoot, to trap and to ferret them. Reuben was now being paid for the same job as he'd previously been fined for doing, and if a pheasant or partridge occasionally found its way into Reuben's bag no one minded now. Micah Elford was finding it increasingly difficult to get supplies of fish, and both he and Mr. Tucker were glad to buy Reuben's victims; what they couldn't sell locally met a ready market in town.

The War Ag set up a machinery depot, tractors, ploughs, cultivators, to work the increased arable acreage. Last Autumn there was only one tractor in the parish and farmers were hard put to get their cultivations done by horses. Old ploughs, harrows, drills, which hadn't been used for many a year were dragged from their nettle beds and hurriedly pressed into service. Large farmers wanted tractors, but they were in short supply, and for this year they would have to be content to hire from the War Ag. Colonel was taken on as a tractor driver, but he'd find the big green Fordson tractor and three furrow plough very different from the pony and little plough he used on his acre. Meanwhile the ground was deeply covered in snow and Colonel assisted Reuben with his rabbit catching.

Uncle George and I sat at the back of the garden shed and lit the oil stove. Uncle sat huddled up close to the stove, spreading his large hands over its flickering top. "Master," he said and sucked in his breath, "master, it's cold and a thick 'un, make no mistake about that. We're in for a long cold spell, you may depend upon that."

He sat there, blowing out his cheeks, wrinkling his brow and muttering "Rajah rhubarb." His face was red from the heat of the stove. He stamped his feet and ordered me to refill the saucepan with cider. I put the saucepan on top of the stove and from a waistcoat pocket Uncle produced a crumpled packet of nutmeg and sprinkled some over the cider. From another pocket he produced ginger and sprinkled that over the cider too, then he stirred it with a finger. "There, boy, that'll make your whiskers curl and keep the cold out, I'll be bound if it won't. Begod, me boy, what wouldn't I give for a bit of tasty cheese, the sort what brings your lips up in blisters. That stuff old Gosworth's selling is no better'n soap. When we go in the house we'll have some boiled onions and pepper and a bit of cold fat bacon."

We drank the remainder of the warm cider. Uncle George smacked his lips and said, "Douse the stove, m'boy, and we'll get on inside in the warm."

It was getting dark and Uncle lit the oil lamp. "The blackouts, me boy, put the blackouts up. I had that durn bobby on to me about showing a chink of light only yesterday and if it ain't him it's that Sam Fisher acawpsing about lights. A bit of orthodoxy 'ave gone to old Sam's yud, soak me bob if it ain't. He's got that officious you casn't live for him and our Aggie thinks he's that wonderful. 'Twas a mistake to give him any orthodoxy — put a beggar on hossback, that's what it is with the old muntle yud. Now the old beggar's on shift work you never know when he's about."

We peeled the onions and put them in a saucepan and Uncle got some cold bacon from the pantry. I put two chrysanthemum-patterned plates and some bone-handled knives and forks on the table.

"Put the kettle to boil and open up the fire," said Uncle. "Pull up a chair and I'll tell you my plans, 'cos while you and young Tom have been a sledging, and Reuben and Colonel have been rabbiting, I've been here alone and I've been doing some thinking in some order."

Uncle filled his pipe and lit it and then, blowing out great clouds of smoke, he stretched out his legs to the fire in the range and said, "We need a Parish Defence Brigade, that's the conclusion I've come to."

"What is a Parish Defence Brigade, Uncle?"

"Durn it, pether, if you'll only keep quiet and listen I'll tell you."

"All right, Uncle."

"It's an idea of my own, a brigade of local able-bodied men to defend the parish, should we have an invasion. Not only for this parish, but for every parish in the kingdom. It's a good idea, ain't it?"

"Oh yes, Uncle, but who's going to start it?"

"Start it? Why, me, of course. As a matter of fact I've started already."

"I haven't heard about it."

"I'm telling you now, ain't I?"

"But why haven't we heard about it if you've already started?"

"Hush, hush, only me and the high ups, the very high ups, know about it yet. I've written to the Speaker of the House of Commons — it's no good writing to the government, they're no bottle. Look at all the trouble I had when I wrote to the Home Secretary about spies — that chap's a proper duffer. But the Speaker is boss of 'em all, they'll have to listen to him."

We ate our boiled onions and bacon and drank our tea. "Something'll be moving soon," said Uncle George, rubbing the side of his nose. "But not a word to anybody, you don't know who's who and what's what these days. Mum's the word about the Parish Defence Brigade."

Days, weeks, went by and Uncle George didn't hear a word about his plans. He grew impatient, despondent and angry. "We'll be invaded by Jerry, my boy. Old Teakle's right, this government is no bloody good. Jerry'll be here, one day we'll see 'em dropping out of the sky as thick as hailstones, you mark my words. Down they'll come in their parryshoots and over-run us, we'll be as defenceless as naked worms. And all those spies who're lying low just now'll rush out and help 'em. If we formed the brigades we could rout out the spies now and be ready to deal with the varmints as they drop out of the sky."

We planted the Epicure early potatoes on the third Sunday in

March. Two days later was market day and Uncle returned earlier than usual. He drove straight to our house in a great state of excitement.

"Boy! Boy! Ethel! Ethel! Confound it, where are you all?" he shouted before he squeezed himself out of the car.

Mother opened the door and peered cautiously out, "Oh dear, it's that George and he's either the worse for drink or else he's finally taken leave of his senses," she said dolefully.

Father came running from the shop to see what all the shouting was about. Mother stood on the doorstep wringing her hands and muttering, "Oh dear, oh dear, what shall I do? I won't have him here, he'll have to be taken away."

But Uncle George only had eyes for me, "C'mon, boy, c'mon quick, jump in the car and come and help me feed the pigs. We've got a helluva lot to do — we've got a busy night before us, a bloody busy night and no mistake. Be quick, jump in — I'll tell you about it on the way." He didn't stop for an answer but ran back to his car.

"You'd better go along with your Uncle," Father told me. "I don't like the looks of him. Keep an eye on him, he don't seem himself."

"No good will come of it, you oughtn't to let him go, Father," said Mother, wringing her apron frantically, but I was already getting in to the car. Uncle drove off violently, crouching over the steering wheel with an intent expression on his face. He was breathing heavily.

"We must feed the pigs and get the hens shut in as quick as possible," he said. "Marcle have got one, Marcle's got one. We must get round as soon as we can. Damn my rags, Marcle have stole a march on us. The buggers'll have to listen to me now. Not for a thousand pun would I have had Marcle put one over us like this."

"What have they got at Marcle, Uncle?"

"Rajah rhubarb, me boy! They've stolen my idea, they've got a brigade. The Marcle Watchers, they call it, but it's my idea, it's a defence brigade. No doubt one of 'em was in The Lion when I was trying to get these bloody nogmen here to form a brigade and they overheard me — or else — " Uncle stopped speaking for a few seconds, sucked his cheeks in and looked pensive, "— or else that Speaker told 'em about it. Perhaps he's got a brother or a cousin living over at Marcle . . . 'pon my soul, I shouldn't have thought the Speaker would have acted like that, you can't depend on anybody these days. Old Teakle have been saying some peculiar things lately, but when something like this happens, it makes you think if there ain't something in what he says — long-headed old fellow Teakle is, for all his funny ways. Anyway, Marcle have got one, eighty strong so I was told today, and we got to do summat here – bloody quick too!"

Uncle shot into the yard and braked viciously. "Get out, me boy, and start mixing the pig grub. I'll just get me smock." I started feeding the squealing, grunting pigs. Uncle bustled about puffing and panting. I think we'd have got on quicker if he hadn't tried to hurry so much, if he'd have been calmer he might not have tripped up by the fowl house.

When the pigs were fed and the hens shut up, Uncle George wiped the beads of sweat from his brow with a large spotted handkerchief, and said, "Right, we'll have a quick cup of tea and a couple of slices of cold mutton and be off."

As we were getting in to the car he said, "We'll do the outliers first." Our first stop was at Mr. Linley's. Mr. Linley was a solid, worthy farmer. His farm was the largest and best managed farm in the district and he employed six or seven men. Mr. Linley listened thoughtfully while Uncle George briefly outlined his plan and asked for Mr. Linley's co-operation and that of his farmworkers. When Uncle George had finished explaining, Mr. Linley said, "I think it's a wonderful idea, but before we do anything, we must get the sanction of the authorities."

"But I've tried, they won't listen. Somebody's got to make a start," said Uncle George.

"You obtain official sanction and I'll back you to the hilt, and see that my chaps do," said Mr. Linley as we left him.

"A good solid chap, Linley, but cautious, too damn cautious. Somebody's got to hack through all the red tape, and, by Harry, I intend to," commented Uncle George when we were back in the car.

We saw Harry Paget, the postman, ahead of us on his bicycle. Uncle George drew alongside him and asked me to open my window. "Hullo there, Harry boy," said Uncle, leaning across me to speak through the open window. "I'm glad I dropped on you, Harry, I'm forming a Parish Defence Brigade." Uncle gave him a few details, Harry leant on the crossbar of his bicycle and listened, his mouth and eyes wide open, dewdrops trickled from the end of his nose and hung from the tips of his thick white moustache like icicles.

"Well, what about it, Harry, be you a gwain to join?"

Harry brushed his nose and moustache with the back of his hand and hitched the postbag up on his shoulder, and after a minute or two, he said, "Well, well, 'tis like this yur, Jarge, be it legal like, do you know?"

"Legal be buggered," snorted Uncle George and drove off in a huff.

We came to Fred Jenkins' cottage. Fred said, yes he'd join, yes, perhaps he'd join, well, yes, he was sure he'd join, ah well, perhaps he would. Mrs. Jenkins came to the door, and planting her fat arms akimbo, said, no, Fred would not join. Fred Jenkins, she said, had a wife and three young children, his duty was to stop at home and defend them. Fred rather sheepishly muttered, "Thank you very much, but I'd rather not join."

"There's no more to be said then, is there?" said Uncle George and we drove on to 'The Villa', home of Mr. Bingle. As we walked up the trim front garden Uncle said, "Bingle's head of the Legion, he'll join like a shot, specially when I tell him about Marcle." But after Uncle had explained carefully, Mr. Bingle wasn't quite sure, he told us he'd have to see what the Legion said about it. "Well," Uncle told him, "don't take too bloody long about it. Jerry won't wait 'til you've finished humming and hawing at British Legion meetings."

Uncle seemed a bit rattled and crashed the gears of his car as we drove off. "The country's strangled in red bloody tape," he complained. We were passing Dr. Frodsham's house (Dr. Frodsham was the retired Doctor who married Mrs. Williams, the lady Uncle had courted briefly a few summers ago).

"What about Dr. Frodsham?" I suggested.

"Him," grunted Uncle. "That little cock-eyed runt wouldn't be any good. I heard he couldn't even aim a hypodermic straight, that's why he had to retire. What good would he be with a gun? He'd be a bloody menace to us all. I'll bet Mrs. Williams knows she's got him, he's as lazy as dung. All he's any good for is tipping sherry down his scrawny little neck. He'd never grow a beetroot for her and she's very fond of a beetroot. Good job there's a high wall round his garden 'cos it's like a wilderness."

"I didn't know you'd been there, Uncle."

"No more have I, but the postman and the butcher have told me 'tis a damned disgrace. You want to keep your eyes and ears open, boy, if you ever want to be as wise as your old Uncle." (Sometime later I happened to mention at home that the Frodshams' garden was wild. "That it never is," said Mother. "That's another of your Uncle's cock and bull stories. They employ a man to do the garden." "So they might, Ethel," said Father, "but that don't mean he's any cop, there's not many as can handle a garden like our George.")

We came to Lionel Collins' small farm. Lionel had a couple of milking cows, a few beef cattle, a dozen breeding ewes and forty or fifty laying hens; though to hear Lionel talk, you'd have thought he had at least a hundred acres, twenty or thirty cows, and goodness knows how many ewes and hens. Lionel had two main topics of conversation, firstly how hard he worked and secondly, the amount of choice fruit his orchard produced — Lionel's fruit was always 'choice' — but his orchard was in a shocking state.

"Be quick, be quick, George, and say what you've gotta say, I'm up to my eyes in work."

Uncle George explained, " — and we need an active young fellow like you, Lionel." Lionel was forty and running to fat.

"Ah, I can see that," said Lionel in his habitual whimsy tone. "I can see you need fellows who know how to shift, and I'd like to help. It's always the willing horses that are needed — of course there's two sorts of willing, the ones like me who are willing to work and the ones who're willing to let 'em."

"Righty-o then," said Uncle. "You'll join?"

"Oh, I'd dearly love to — but I haven't the time, I'm up to my eyes, don't know which way to turn. I'm on from daylight to dark, it'll be the death of me, all the work. If people only knew — but there's so much to be done and only me to do it, I can't let up for a moment."

"So you won't join?"

"Not won't, George, can't — I haven't time to scratch my bottom I've so much to do. I just simply haven't the time — people just don't realise how hard I work."

"Good-day to you then, Lionel, we won't waste any more of your precious time," said Uncle George, slamming the car door shut.

"If people only knew how hard I worked, I've so much to do, I haven't time to scratch my bottom," mimicked Uncle George, assuming Lionel's whimsy voice and petulant expression, and then reverting to his own deep voice, "The lazy bugger's allus sat on his arse, that's why he can't scratch it. He's never done a day's work in his life. God knows what he'll do when he retires, he'll never know the difference. But rajah rhubarb, can't he boast and moan! Hard work'll never kill him, he ain't goin' to give it the chance, he'll rust out, not wear out."

We saw Reuben walking across a field; we could only just see him, it was beginning to get dark. Uncle hailed him.

After a few minutes explanation Reuben said, "Of course I'll join, George, and so will old Colonel, it'll be like old times for him, Colonel'll be a very useful man to have."

"Good man," said a beaming Uncle George. "I knew I could rely on you and old Colonel. Colonel ought to be a very handy chap in a scrap — I'll let you know the arrangements as soon as I've made em."

Reuben waved goodbye and Uncle said to me, "We'll call on Major

Mostyn now. I'll let him be leader as he's a retired military man, he should know the ropes."

However, Major Mostyn wasn't enthusiastic. "Dammit all, man, we can't have every Tom, Dick or Harry wandering around with firearms. The police should have confiscated all shotguns before now. These are funny times. Most undesirable for the lower classes to have weapons unless they're under the strictest discipline. Very dangerous, most unsettled times, lot of Bolshie talk about, don't you know. Sorry old man, know you mean well and all that, but must be realistic don't you know."

As we approached the village Uncle George said, "There'll be no more eggs for the Major."

"What about Mr. Elford?" I asked.

"Dammit all, boy, he's no good, he's as yellow as a guinea — look how he yelled when his missus tickled his arse with them 'ettles, just think what he'd do if he saw a Jerry. And he'd give the show away if he was lying low in ambush, Jerry'd smell that stinking old fish on him."

"Peabody?"

"Soft as pap and I wouldn't put any dependence in Banstead, the man's a damn fool; Teakle's too old, Ludgater might turn up trumps and so might a few more like Eddy and Davie."

We saw Farmer Wilson in the High Street. "Hey there, Len," shouted Uncle. Mr. Wilson said he'd join, but if the invasion came at haymaking time not to rely on him.

Alfred Tucker the butcher seemed keen, because he said he'd slit any Jerry's throat, brigade or no brigade. Emmanuel Fowler who'd been Tucker's delivery man since Mr. Farquharson had dismissed him, had to be counted out, he was now engaged full time in the Fire Service. "Fowler would have been a useful chap," said Uncle George. "Lord, how he's changed."

We knocked on Mr. Gosworth's door and told him of our mission. "Just a minute, I'll see what the wife says," he said, and popped back into the house leaving the door ajar. We stood on the doorstep and heard what Mrs. Gosworth had to say — "No, Leonard, you will do no such thing. Parish Defence Brigade indeed, Parish Boozing Brigade if that George has anything to do with it. Booze, booze, booze, that's all it would be, and I'm not having you come back here drunk. Get rid of the wretched man, tell him you'll have nothing to do with it."

Mr. Gosworth came back to the door and said, "I'm not sure one way or the other, I'll think it over and let you know in a week or two."

"Huh," said Uncle George, "Len Gosworth ain't much of a man, nor much of a grocer either."

"Yus, yus, yus," said Amos Bloxham when we asked him. "Oho yus, and leave my wife here at nights to cock 'er arse to all and sundry, oho yus, a bloody fine caper that'd be 'ouldn't it?"

Uncle George and I went home. "Soak me bob, boy 'tis no bottle, we ain't got the response we should have. We need every able manjack on a job like this. It's very disappointing, but we've done our best. Nobody can say we ain't tried because we have, and that's the great thing, to try. Most of the buggers wun't try, give 'em a drop of beer in the bottom of a bucket and then they'll lie down and snore like hogs. I don't know as old Sam Fisher's the worst on'em after all, he do persevere with his raids. We may as well call it a day."

During the following weeks Uncle George and I got on with the garden, we planted peas, shallots, onions and earthed the early potatoes up. We planted the maincrop potatoes and got the ground ready for the runner beans.

We saw Colonel driving a tractor on various farms, and we helped him plant his acre with potatoes.

The war news got worse and at last a coalition government was formed; Mr. Churchill became Prime Minister, but Mr. Teakle's enthusiasm was lukewarm. He remarked, "The bungling of Churchill over Norway has caused the downfall of Chamberlain, and Churchill is made Prime Minister." Mr. Teakle never shared the general adulation of Churchill and his criticism of the great man in the coming months and years made him rather unpopular, and even worse was his praise for Aneurin Bevan.

Father said he was afraid Teakle was turning into a damned agitator; others said, he's no Liberal, he's a Socialist, or even a Bolshie. Mrs. Hatch who could always be relied upon to go too far, called him a traitor.

"Mr. Lloyd George would have been the man to do the job, but alas, he's an old man, his powers are failing — when I think of the young Mr. Lloyd George — what a reformer he was — but there is a young Welshman who will one day continue the great work started by Mr. Lloyd George."

"But, Mr. Teakle, Father says that man is an agitator," I replied.

"So was Mr. Lloyd George once."

"But Father and other people say he's a trouble maker, a dreadful man."

"That's what people once said about Mr. Lloyd George, now they call him a great man. I may not live to see the day when Bevan is called a great man, but you will, and you will remember my words." People shook their heads over Mr. Teakle.

But Uncle George and I scorned all politicians and kept our energies for the garden and pigs and, of course, Uncle was kept busy with his lectures.

However, it was a pity that Uncle George had no wireless, because he missed Eden's speech asking for Local Defence Volunteers. The first Uncle knew about it was when he collected his *Daily Mail* from Mrs. Hatch next morning. It was Uncle's idea after all, and I would have liked him to have been the first to rush down to the Police Station to volunteer.

They made Major Mostyn leader — well, if they didn't know the sort of man Major Mostyn was, Uncle George and I did.

Chapter 13

TO THE BARRICADES!

AFTER the Eden broadcast, Uncle George made a habit of coming to our house to listen to the news, most evenings he came to hear either the six o'clock or the nine o'clock news. He even got bold enough to twiddle the knobs and turn on to the Forces Programme, much to Mother's annoyance, because she wouldn't allow Father or me to touch the wireless, it was hers. But if Uncle George wanted to do anything, not even Mother could stop him. She'd go red in the face, she'd glare at him, but Uncle George took no notice except to remark, "You seem a bit irritable tonight, Ethel, are you a bit out of sorts?"

Uncle became quite addicted to some programmes. Rob Wilton was his favourite comedian ("The day war broke out I was in The Red Lion." "And I," Uncle would reply, "was in The White Lion"). He was vastly amused by the antics of Tommy Handley, Fusspot and Fumf. Mother would not stop in the room when the Handley programme was on, and every time Uncle George laughed, Father would scowl and shake his head. Father could see nothing funny in the programme, it was for townspeople, he said, and townspeople were daft enough to laugh at anything, and he began to fear that Uncle George was going soft in the head.

Then Uncle George discovered Mr. Middleton and his Sunday afternoon gardening talks. After Sunday dinner he'd settle down to listen to Mr. Middleton. "In the most comfortable chair, the cratur," Mother said. "When I've been slaving over a hot oven, working my fingers to the bone to fill the cratur's great canister. He eats like a pig, then gets indigestion and makes those disgusting noises. It's because of those disgusting noises my sister won't come to stop with us, my only sister, and I can't have her to stay with me because of that object."

From the look on Uncle George's face while he listened to Mr. Middleton, you could see it was one expert listening to another. "Good afternoon," said Mr. Middleton. "Good afternoon," said Uncle George. Then Uncle George would lean forward in his chair and cup his hand to his ear; even Mother would not dare to speak until Mr. Middleton was finished. From time to time Uncle George would nod his head in agreement or purse his lips and wrinkle his brow in disagreement. When the programme was over, Uncle George would give his comments, "Very good today a lot of common sense," or, "Didn't hardly hold with what he said about beetroot." He also gave his opinion about the broadcaster's health, "He didn't sound very well today," or "Asthmatical, I should say." Months later it was, "I think his health is failing, I hope he's got a good doctor, otherwise, it's all taboo with him, you know." I noticed, but didn't understand, the gleam in Uncle George's eye every time he said Mr. Middleton's health was failing.

Afterwards Father and Uncle discussed the topics in the *News of the World;* doctors, the weather and, usually, some miraculous remedy Uncle George was going to purchase the very next time he was in town. The discourse would only be interrupted by Father shouting, "Oh, Ethel, make us a pot of tea, we're that dry, and bring our George a biscuit if you have one."

"One Sunday when you shout for tea, I'll be gone" Mother once told him, "I'll have packed my bags, put on my hat and coat and gone. Gone and shaken the dust of this place off my feet. Any why? I'll tell you why, because I'm sick, sorry and tired of being at your beck and call."

"If you haven't any biscuits, a couple of those little Welsh cakes you made yesterday would be very nice," said Father.

"You didn't listen to a word I said."

"Oh yes I did, Ethel, but you don't mean a word of it, my dear," said Father in soothing tones.

"Don't you be too sure of that," answered Mother.

One Sunday, when Mother brought the cups of tea in, Uncle George drew her aside and said to her kindly, "Ethel, I've brought something that'll interest you." He put his hand in his jacket pocket. "At your time of life," he suddenly looked very solemn, "you should be taking medicine – ah, ah now, I know, I have, as you know, a certain amount of medical knowledge." He rummaged about in his pocket, "I've got it here somewhere, you should be taking medicine. Ah, here it is." He handed her a folded piece of paper, "It's an advertisement for the stuff you need. When I saw it, I thought, that's just what Ethel wants."

Mother unfolded the paper, took a brief glance at it and then screwed it up and flung it into the fire. "I've never been so humiliated in all my life," she cried, and with a bitter look at Father she said, "How you can sit there and let him say such things to me I don't know. I shall go clean out of my mind if I have to put up with any more of it." She quickly left the room and we heard her running upstairs.

"I can't understand what's come over her" said Father.

"You're going to have a job with her," Uncle George told him.

$$* \quad * \quad * \quad *$$

The fall of France, Dunkirk. "We're all done for," said Ronald Ferneyhough.

"What about Formby and the Maginot Line now?" asked Father.

"We shall win, we always do, because we're in the right," said Mrs. Hatch.

Farmers were told to build their hayricks in the middle of fields to help prevent enemy aircraft landing, and the grass verges at the roadsides were left uncut as camouflage. Stinging nettles were needed for medicinal purposes; "At last Micah can do something useful," commented Uncle George, looking over the hedge at Elford's large clumps of nettles.

A man from the War Ag was calling on all farmers to see that they cut their docks and thistles. "He has his pockets full of dock and thistle seed and sows 'em wherever he goes," said Len Wilson, "to ensure that his cushy job is safe." Farmers complained that many of the War Ag Officials were 'broken down farmers', 'ne'r do wells,' the sort who never could make a go of it themselves, and now they're telling us what to do. The War Ag had taken over a one hundred and fifty acre farm in the district, and were running it themselves, and it was reputed to be the worst run farm in the area.

Some farmers' wives became jealous of the amount of time and attention their husbands spent with the landgirls.

Sam Fisher said that the strain of the work and responsibility of it was beginning to tell on his health. His heads, he said, were, "summat cruel," and his back was, "playing up like nobody's business."

* * * *

The L.D.V. were issued with uniforms, and armbands with the letters L.D.V. They now had a motley collection of weapons which ranged from Major Mostyn's old army pistol to shotguns and pikes. In his garden shed the Major had a large collection of bottles filled with petrol, the celebrated Molotov Cocktails. A local timber factory had turned out a lot of wooden bottles, and most evenings the L.D.V. practised throwing them and drilled with broom and pike handles. They also took every roll of barbed wire that Father had in stock.

Zebrina Ellicot returned to The Rose and Crown, accompanied by her husband and baby daughter, her husband looking very dashing in R.A.F. Pilot's uniform. Mr. Trophimus Ellicot hung up a picture of Churchill behind the bar, and took to wearing a bow tie and smoking cigars. The villagers called him Winnie the Pooh.

* * * *

The danger of invasion was imminent and Churchill said, "We shall defend every village." Our L.D.V. set up barricades at all entrances to our village. Everyone seemed to think the Germans would come down the hill, know as the 'Deep Cutting' because of the high banks of rock on either side of the road, which presumably had once had to be cut through to form the road. Big ash trees grew on top of the

98

banks, their exposed roots twisting over the rock face. I watched the preparation for the barricade being made there.

Back in February Uncle George had foreseen the dangers of invasion, but nobody had listened to him; but now everybody was talking of invasion, so I was glad to see that Uncle George was in charge, though it was apparent that Major Mostyn thought that he was, and becoming a great hindrance. Uncle George put up with the Major's interference for a considerable time, but at last he could stand it no longer and spoke quite sharply.

"Now look here, Major, stand back and let the dog see the rabbit. Now, men, we must get a gurt ellum trunk and wrap plenty of barb wire round 'un and fix'n on a pivot — I hope you all know what a pivot is — and then when Jerry comes, us can flop'n down over the road — flop, like that!" Uncle brought one large hand down on top of the other and looked at his men fiercely. "Good, good, now we've got that straight. We'll get one from the timber yard directly — here you, Reuben, you just run sharp along to old Winkleberry, the manager, and tell him to have a timber lorry and a gurt ellum ready." He paused for a moment and then went on, "Now, now, Major, you just stand back and let them as do know do the talking. I've got all this organised as you'd see if you'd only stop fidgeting and listen. I've got it all fathomed out down to the smallest detail. And up thur, men," Uncle made a magnificent gesture and pointed to a large ash tree, "I want a hideout built." He paused here to allow his words to sink in. Even the Major stopped fussing to look and listen. "And then when Jerry comes," Uncle raised his voice, "I'll be there with a gun and some of them Mollytoff Cocks to chuck at 'em." Uncle paused again, chuckled and said in a lower voice, "Ah, and maybe I'll have a bottle or two of parsnip wine." Then raising his voice and waving an arm, "And I'll fight to the last drop of blood, the last ounce of breath in me body — ," he glared fiercely, "and I shall expect all you buggers to do the same."

"I'd aim old Jarge'll do most of his fightin' in The Lion," said Fred Pollard nastily.

Of course the trouble with Fred Pollard was jealousy, because Uncle swept the deck at the Show every year. Pollard was big-headed, he was never willing to learn, he thought he already knew everything. He'd never attended any of Uncle's lectures and I once said to his son Cedric, "Why doesn't your Father come to the gardening talks?" to which the cocky little begger replied, "Huh! My Dad's forgot more'n your Uncle ever learnt about gardening."

All the Pollards are the same, cocky and ignorant with it. I shall never forget the time old Simpky rapped Cedric's knuckles. She only did it once, Cedric screamed and screamed and Mrs. Pollard came to the school and made a fuss and told Simpky that old Fred was going to report her. All the Pollards make a fuss, and then collapse like a pricked balloon. Fred Pollard did, when Uncle spoke out to him about his remark at the barricade about doing his fighting in The Lion.

"I heard what you said, Fred Pollard, and if I have any more of your insubordination, I'll lambast you, I'll put you in hospital for a month or more."

Then Major Mostyn stepped in and began to show his authority. He was leader of the L.D.V., he said, and he couldn't allow this sort of brawling. Uncle George humoured him and let him get on with it, but, later, when we were alone, Uncle told me that Mostyn was a fool and he'd half a mind not to let him have any more eggs.

Chapter 14

OF GOOD AND ILL

THE L.D.V. became the Home Guard. They changed the uniform and instead of armbands reading L.D.V. they now had armbands bearing the letters H.G. Uncle George never joined the Home Guard. Major Mostyn said it was because he was too old, but Uncle said that he had too many other commitments. Anyway, Major Mostyn had no eggs for a month.

*   *   *   *

The Fruit, Flower and Vegetable show was cancelled. Micah Elford couldn't get much fish and not enough vegetables either. He came and asked Uncle George to sell him some and Uncle told him, "Afore the war you didn't want my vegetables, no, and I didn't want your stinking old fish neither. Now you ain't got much fish and you ain't agwain to have my beautiful vegetables. I can sell all my fruit and vegetables without your help."

"Oh very well, George, if that's the way you feel about it, but remember there'll be another day," said Micah Elford.

"You should have thought of that when you told me you didn't want my vegetables afore the war," said Uncle George.

"Times was different then, George."

"Ah, so they might have bin, and you've got a different story for these times, but my story's the same. I didn't want your stinking old fish afore the war and I don't want it now."

"Oh, that's the way it is, is it? I was only trying to do you a good turn, George," said Elford and walked away.

"Ah that's the way it is, and that's the way it's a gwain to stop, Micah," said Uncle George.

"Mr. Churchill is a better man than Mr. Chamberlain," said Mrs. Peabody. "When the King asked Mr. Chamberlain to have a national day of prayer he said, no, but when the King asked Mr. Churchill he agreed."

"We should be all right now then, now that we've conscripted God," commented Mr. Teakle dryly.

Edward Jones heard that his son Bert had been captured at Dunkirk and was a Prisoner of War in Germany. A conscientious objector came to work on Mr. Linley's farm.

"Mr. Linley ought to be ashamed of himself, harbouring a conchie," said Mrs. Hatch. "All conchies ought to be made to join the army or be locked up. If that conchie dared to come in to this shop, I'd tell him what I thought of him. He ought to be shot."

"It is democracy and freedom we're supposed to be fighting for," answered Mr. Teakle.

"Then why ain't that conchie fightin' for it?" snorted Mrs. Hatch.

Several stray bombs dropped in the parish, but nobody was injured and little damage was done. One dropped quite near the village, in a field at the bottom of the Lloyd/Heckitt gardens and both families had their windows blown out. After they'd recovered from the initial shock, they began to accuse each other.

"We should never have had that bomb drop on us, if she hadn't been quatting in the garden with a fag in her mouth," Mrs. Heckitt said.

"She'd cleaned the copper out and left hot ashes glowing in the garden," said Mrs. Lloyd.

"We could all have bin killed through her and her fag."

"It was lucky we wasn't all killed in our beds through her and her careless ways."

The excitement of the bomb died down, and we had no more dropped locally. The war once again seemed remote to me, though not perhaps to Zebrina, pushing her daughter down the High Street while her husband was fighting the Battle of Britain. Not to Mr. Bence who had a grandson on a minesweeper, nor to Mr. Teakle, who didn't know where his son was, nor to others with husbands and sons in the forces.

But Mr. Teakle continued to talk of tolerance, and Mr. Bence preached love and forgiveness from his pulpit. The others said little about the war and busied themselves about their daily tasks.

Mrs. Hatch preached patriotism at her shop, but would not allow her daughter to do any war work. Davie and Eddy Bridges were called up. "A bit of discipline will do those two the world of good," declared Mrs. Hatch. The two younger porters at the station were also called up and our trains were packed with soldiers, sailors and airmen travelling from and to 'somewhere in England'.

*   *   *

We had a series of thefts in the village; ladies underwear was snatched from clothes lines. "I'd aim half the women of this village are walking about without any drawers," said Uncle George. "Have you lost your bloomers, Ethel?" he asked one Sunday afternoon when Mother brought the cups of tea. "Perhaps it's because of the shortage, but it must be more than one person doing it, cos the person who wanted them great drawers that Fred Jenkins' wife do wear'd never be able to get into the tiny things that'd fit Mrs. Peabody's scrawny arse."

"I'm not stopping here to listen to you going into detail about the size and shape of every woman's figure in the parish, George, it's not decent for a bachelor to talk about such things," said Mother, putting the cups down on the table with a clatter and spilling some of the tea.

"Steady, steady, Ethel, old lady," said Father.

"Don't you old lady me, and when I've washed up I hope both of you will clear out, I want to listen to Sandy on my wireless."

"Or else it's somebody stealing 'em an' selling 'em on the black market," said Uncle George, returning to the mystery of the missing knickers when Mother had departed.

"There's some bad baggers about, George," said Father.

"Or we've got a queer 'un round about. There's old Amos, he's an odd sort of chap."

"There's some funny baggers about, George."

"Or they'm a wearin' them theirselves. There's Lionel Collins, always wondered if he were a bit of a will-jill."

"Here," Father said to me, "go and give your poor Mother a bit of a hand with the washing up; this is no sort of talk for a lad."

* * *

Lionel Collins had more things to worry about than knickers; the War Ag had ordered him to plough up ten acres of pasture. He complained bitterly to everyone he saw, "Ten acres, yes, ten acres. I don't know how I'll manage and they won't listen to reason. Ten acres, they say, and it must be planted with wheat this winter. I told them it simply couldn't be done, I haven't the time, I haven't even got a plough. Don't worry, they said, we'll come and plough it and plant it. Goodness knows what they'll charge. You'll get two pounds an acre for ploughing up, they said. But I told them, there's all the work, all the work of harvesting and threshing — they simply don't understand. I'd never have bought those geese if I'd known."

Emmanuel Fowler left us, for London and the blitz, where he subsequently earned a medal for bravery, and Uncle George said, when he heard about the reward, "We did the right thing the day we burnt a handkerchief, boy."

Colonel harvested his potatoes and sold them. He bought a motorbike as he had to travel long distances now, ploughing, harvesting and so on. This was the first time he'd made a profit from his acre and had strangely lost interest in it; he had no plans for next year's cropping and talked vaguely of letting the acre.

* * *

Sam Fisher was suffering from the strain of work and the shortage of acid drops. He bought up a stock of liquorice root to help him to keep going, and always had black saliva trickling over his chin.

The day I called on Aunt Aggie I found her near tears. "Your poor Uncle Sam is cracking up," she said. I saw an open copy of *Dene Hollow* by Mrs. Henry Wood at her side, and suspected that the book, as well as the state of her husband's health, had brought her to tears. She had a bookcase full of novels by Mrs. Henry Wood and Marie Corelli; *The Constant Nymph* and *If Winter Comes* were also there. She often read them and had a weep. "I do enjoy a good book" she said, but Mother called them a lot of trash.

* * * *

"Give me the boot, quick, Reuben," said Uncle George. Reuben handed Uncle the old boot with the toe cut off and Uncle rammed it down the sow's squealing mouth. "Pigs have got a mouth full of tith," said Uncle as I handed him the bottle of medicine. "You sure you got a slip knot in that rope, Reuben?" The sow was straining back on the rope tied to her jaw, the other end to a post in the shed, she was 'out of sorts' and Uncle was drenching her. Colonel was there too, but he couldn't help, he'd recently discovered that a combination of motorbike, cider and icy roads was dangerous, he'd fallen off the bike and broken his arm.

After Uncle had poured the mixture down the sow's throat, he pulled the loose end of rope by her snout and she ran off grunting, and shaking her head, her large ears flap-flapping. "That'll do you a power of good, old girl," said Uncle.

The four of us went into the cider house.

You've made a devil of a lot of cider this year, George," said Colonel.

"Oh, it'll be needed, you'll see," said Uncle as he filled a large mug.

"What you going to grow on your field next year, Colonel?" asked Reuben.

"I don't know, thee casn't grow spuds two year running cast? I might let'n out for a year or two."

"Dussent want to do that," said Reuben.

"Grow swedes," said Uncle.

"This is a drop of good, by jove if it ain't," said Colonel, drinking from the mug and smacking his lips.

"D'y'ever know me make any bad cider, Colonel?" asked Uncle.

"No, no, all cider's good, but some's better'n others," said Colonel, and took another good pull at the mug.

"Come on Colonel, pass the cup round," said Reuben.

"The boy do like his drop of cider, don't he?" asked Colonel.

"Do Mrs. Peabody still go to the spinney?" asked Colonel.

"You'd wonder what sort of chap 'ould fancy a skinng 'oman like her," said Uncle.

"Nearer the bone, they do say," said Colonel.

"I'd aim there's a lot of that sort of thing going on at these yer factories, chaps and wenches working together," said Reuben.

"D'you think old Sam's a doin' it?" asked Colonel.

"No, not old Sam," said Uncle. "He's too slow and lazy."

"He do stick that job in the factory, though," said Colonel.

"Case of he bloody got to," answered Uncle.

"They got all us old odd jobbers a working steady now," said Colonel.

"Bad job about poor old Trump, they oughtn't to turn a poor harmless old man out like that," said Uncle.

"No, it's shameful," said Colonel.

"But you can't have land lay idle," said Reuben.

"I never said you could, Reuben, but his land ain't lay idle, t'aint the best of land, the owld chap needed a bit of help, that twere all; t'ain't a very big place, anyhow. From what I hear, they'm wasting that amount up at the War Ag place," said Uncle.

"Ah, that's right enough, what with their roads and yups of rotting straw. I said to the supervisor, byunt you a gwain to get that straw shifted and all them old staddles tidied up so's I can plough," said Colonel. "And he said, there's plenty for you to plough — get on with it and mind your own business."

"Ah, and what corn ricks be left is riddled with rats. I can't keep 'em down," said Reuben.

"Yur 'tis January, and all the ground ain't planted," grumbled Colonel.

"Claude Linley's going to speak about it at the Farmers' meeting, he don't like the way they've served the old chap," said Uncle.

"If Mr. Linley says it's wrong, then it's wrong," said Colonel.

"Claude Linley told me himself," said Uncle George, "I know we must grow every ounce of food we can, but I still don't approve of the way they've acted over Trump and I heard Dan Teakle say in The Lion, in fighting for freedom we must not forget what freedom is. Dan Teakle said that, and Claude Linley heard him and agreed."

"Teakle's a funny old chap, but he's longheaded," said Reuben.

"They'll have to take note of what Claude Linley do say, he's a mighty man. He used to be Chairman of the Farmers' Union and of the Conservatives — he's got a bit of pull, mind," said Uncle.

"Very highly respected man," said Reuben.

"Claude Linley's one of the best. Best farmer for miles around and good to his men. Everybody speaks highly of Linley. Old Dan Teakle don't always see eye to eye with him, as you know, but Dan allus had a high opinion of Linley," said Uncle.

"They'll have to listen to Mr. Linley," said Colonel

"Mr. Linley will speak out to the point," said Reuben.

*   *   *   *

When Uncle and I went into the house, Aunt Aggie was there. "I've brought you a nice bit of fish from town, George," she said; and to me: "And how's your Mother?" "She's very well Auntie, thank you." "I don't see very much of her these days — not since she was so nasty about my Sam."

"Oh bury the axe, Aggie, let bygones be bygones," said Uncle George.

"It hurt me very much, hearing she'd been round the town saying nasty things about my Sam."

"It was a long time ago, Aggie — forget it," said Uncle.

"It hurt me deeply, to think my own brother's wife should say such things."

"Put the kettle on, Aggie, and say no more about it, I don't expect she meant it."

"It cut me — to think anybody should say such things about my poor old Sam."

"I expect Ethel was feeling a bit out of sorts at the time — time of life, you know."

"I've no wish to be bad friends. Tell your Mother I'll come and see her one day."

"How's Sam, Aggie?"

"I'm afraid the poor old fellow's feeling the strain, but he won't give up. No, my Sam's not the sort to give up easily."

"Give him a drop of whisky to buck him up."

"I try to keep a drop in the house, but it's hard to come by nowadays."

"I'll see if I can get you a drop from Mrs. Sackville when I go into town."

"Sam's suffering from metal fatigue. Dr. Higgins says he must wear glasses."

"I thought he'd got glasses."

"That's right."

"Well?"

"Ah, but he hasn't wore them. Now the Doctor says he must wear them."

"How long's he had glasses?"

"Ever since he saw the Doctor about his bad heads and the Doctor sent him to the Optician two or three year ago."

"Yes, I should think it's about time he wore them then."

"That's what the Doctor said, but poor old Sam didn't understand."

"I hope he understands now."

"Oh yes, I went to the Doctor with him."

"Is he any better?"

"He misses his acid drops and that liquorice stuff he keeps chewing makes such a mess everywhere and he spits the chewed up stuff out all over the place, but I don't say anything to the poor old fellow."

107

"You looking after yourself, Aggie, taking medicine?"

"Oh yes, George. I take phyllosan and bile beans every day and iron tablets, and a mixture once a week besides a pinch of epsom salts in my early morning tea."

"That should be all right to be going on with, Aggie."

"And Sam has his Doans' and I rub liniment into the poor old fellow's back most nights, or days. Of course with this shifty business, we don't know what's day and what's night, poor old Sam and me. And I think that canteen food he gets gives him the stoppage something terrible. Mind he tries, I can hear him in the privy, grunting and straining, you can't say the poor old fellow don't try. I give him Andrews' but he won't drink it when it's fizzy. I say to him, I say, Sam, to get the benefit you must drink it while it fizzes, but it gets up his poor old nose and I don't like to grumble at him. If only he'd have a pinch of Epsoms in his tea like me, but he don't like it, he don't like it at all."

"Try him with senna, Aggie. I've got a few pods I can let you have to start him on, but mind you, he must persevere with it. And as soon as ever I've got some rhubarb I'll let you have some, that'll loosen him up."

"I've got some dirty socks and a shirt, vest and pants in my bag, George, to take home and wash for you."

"Thank you, Aggie, and for the fish."

"You seen Amos Bloxham's face, George? Oh, it isn't half a mess."

"What's he been doing, fighting with Bonnor again?"

"No, Bonnor won't go up to the house now. He leaves the milk at the garden gate ever since Amos set about him. No, Amos fell off his bike right outside my place." Aunt Aggie's face began to crease. If you didn't know her you'd think she was about to cry, but in fact she was laughing. "I know it was awful, I oughtn't to laugh, but he looked so funny, his feet flying up into the air, I had to laugh. I know it was awful, but I like a good laugh. When Sam isn't too tired he sings me a comic song and I have a good laugh. Most days he says, I'll sing you one of my songs, Aggie, it'll do you good. No, Sam, I say, not if you're too tired, but the old dear says, it'll do you good, Aggie, you know how you love a good laugh."

"Kind of him," said Uncle.

"Oh Sam's that kind. Can you let me have a few eggs to cook for the old fellow's tea."

"Certainly, Aggie, and a bit of bacon."

"No, thank you, George, no bacon. Sam can't eat any fat, it makes him queasy — he's got such a delicate tummy — Goodness!

108

Look at the time! If I don't get off home, I shan't have his tea ready and everything comfy for him."

"Here's the eggs, Aggie, and a drop of parsnip wine."

"Oh thank you, George," said Aunt Aggie, and turning to me she said, "Remember me to your Mother and tell her I'll be round to see her if I'm welcome and don't forget to tell her your Uncle Sam's poorly."

"No wonder," said Uncle when we were having tea, "our Aggie looks so miserable if she's got to listen to one of old Sam's songs every day."

Chapter 15

HE'S DRIVING ME OUT OF MY MIND –

WHEN the Radio Doctor began to broadcast, Uncle George soon got to hear about him and started coming down to listen, stopping on to breakfast. "He's driving me out of my mind," said Mother. "He's here every whip stitch."

Mother complained about the number of meals Uncle George ate at our house. "That man is eating us out of house and home, and I'm working my fingers to the bone for the cratur. He comes and squats here with his morbid talk of illness and doctors and murder and I have to wait on him hand, foot and finger."

"Now, now, Ethel," Father remonstrated, "he's very good to us, look at all the bacon he brings."

"Huh! You'd have something to say if I gave you that nasty old salt muck. He never brings it until it's gone too rancid to eat, it's all yellow and green and even the dog won't look at it."

"But his eggs are all right."

"Well, yes, – but every one I crack I expect to be bad."

"And his vegetables are good."

Mother nodded her head and Father pressed his advantage, "And his fruit and honey and firewood." Mother had to agree. "I'm glad that for once you can't find fault with our George," said Father triumphant.

"Sprats to catch mackerels!" replied Mother and flounced out of the room.

Uncle George thoroughly enjoyed the Radio Doctor's broadcasts. "That man," he said, "is first class, down to earth, no nonsense about him. He knows what he's talking about; I've advised Dr. Higgins to listen to him. I've a damn good mind to write and ask him to have a look at poor old Middleton, that man's going back fast."

"Pour our George another cup of tea, Ethel my dear," said Father.

"How're you getting on with your First Aid Classes, Ethel?" asked Uncle George. "The district nurse told me that old Frodsham's a proper old fuzzle-buzzle, got no idea how to do a bandage."

"He's a real gentleman, he doesn't use vulgar expressions. I can't understand the B.B.C. allowing it," said Mother.

"It's a lot of nonsense," said Father, glancing up from a letter he was reading. "It isn't true and it isn't funny. They'll laugh at anything. There's one fellow who's there every time, I recognise his laugh; I can't understand why they put on such rubbish. Then there's that squawking woman, they've got her on all the time."

"I was talking about the Radio Doctor," Mother explained, "with all his vulgar talk about bellies and bowels and grub. Just after Christmas he was talking about constipation and said that after too much food the body says, 'What I have I hold'. Visit the throne whether you like it or not, he said. I felt myself go hot all over. When we were girls we were taught not to talk about such things."

"If you are starting to go hot all over, Ethel, you ought to go and see Dr. Higgins," said Uncle George.

"Why can't they have some of the good old songs?" asked Father. "Real singers like Vesta Tilley. The noise that squawking woman makes ain't singing, it puts my teeth on edge."

"I like Sandy best," said Mother.

"I've got as I like a bit of wireless," said Uncle George.

"If you're so fond of the wireless, I can't understand why you don't buy one of your own," snapped Mother.

"Oh I would, Ethel, I'd dearly like one of my own, but you can't get them for love or money now — and I ain't got love nor money," said Uncle in a forlorn voice.

"Huh!" said Mother when Uncle George had gone. "That George is stinking with money, he's making money hand over fist." She began to clear the breakfast and then went on, "Because beer's short he sold all that watery old cider — never known that George so fond of water before. And the vegetables and the fruit, he's raking the money in. But, being George, he's not content, oh no, he's in thick on the black market now."

There was something in what Mother said. Uncle George was doing well and illegally selling eggs and pigmeat to The George in town. He once had his car stall when the boot was stuffed full of illicit goods, so he hailed a couple of burly policemen standing close by. "I'm afraid my car's conked, just give me a push round the corner into the yard of The George, will you?"

"It's only little pigs, Ethel, small porkers, and he only kills them when there's an r in the month," said Father.

"The authorities wouldn't see it that way if he got caught. And what about Dorothea and her husband in the bank? The worry of it all will drive me clean out of my mind."

"What about them silk stockings he got for you, then? You didn't seem to take the same attitude over them, did you?" But Mother had gone to wash the dishes.

Despite the continual complaints from Mother, which Father tactfully ignored, Uncle George continued to make frequent calls to listen to the wireless and to regale our mealtimes with local gossip and commentaries on radio programmes. During harvest time he told us of the scandal about Mr. Wilson and the landgirls.

"It's a cock and bull story, I don't believe a word of it," said Mother. "Mr. Wilson is not a man like that."

"Of course he is, Ethel," said Uncle George. "Look how he goes to them dances, and in his dirty wellingtons, too."

"I don't see what his dirty wellingtons have got to do with it," Mother replied.

"Precious little as far as I can see, from what I hear he gets up to, apart from the fact that he's wearing 'em," said Uncle.

"I can't believe it," said Mother.

"It's a true bill all right as you're bound to know, Ethel. You go to the whist drives, don't you?"

"You know I do."

"Well, hasn't Len Wilson ever put his hand on your knee?"

"He certainly has not," said Mother indignantly.

"Well he's felt nearly every other woman's knee, and put his hand up their skirts. They do say as Mrs. Peabody don't even flinch, she do like it, they say, change from the spinney, I suppose."

"Father, Father, how can you sit there and let him say such things?"

"What's that you say, my dear?" asked Father.

"You turn a deaf ear, don't you?" she snorted.

On the wireless they started to play the National Anthem, Mother immediately jumped up and stood rigidly to attention — she'd been doing this regularly for quite six months now.

"Now, now Ethel, I've told you before, there's no need for that," Father told her.

"It shows respect and loyalty," said Mother when the Anthem had stopped.

"Well I say there's no need to do that sort of job, not in your own home, you only do that when people can see you."

"You three here saw me do it, and you three ought to have done it too," Mother said.

"Well, I ain't going to start bobbing up and down like a jack-in-the-box in me own home every time them fellows on the wireless starts playing God Save the King. What do you say, George?"

"I'm nicely settled, it'd upset me belly to keep jumping up like Ethel do," said Uncle.

"You've got no respect, either of you, and it sets a bad example," Mother told them.

"I respect the King," said Uncle George.

"What'd you call the King if you was to meet him, George?" asked Father.

"I'd call him Your Majesty."

"So would I, that's what I told Pemberthy, but no, he said you call the King Sire. I told him that's what you call a bull or a stallion."

"Ah well, he's going back to King Edward VII's time, I expect," said Uncle George.

That Sunday's conversation must have rankled Mother, as she was still complaining bitterly about Uncle George the following day, more bitterly than usual.

"It was bad enough when we had him squatting here all day on Sundays, then he started coming here most evenings, and now he's here before breakfast in the mornings. The cratur's here morning, noon and night, it's more than flesh and blood can stand. Why doesn't he go to that Aggie's instead, why should I have to be saddled with the wretch? And that Aggie sending me messages about Sam Fisher being poorly, not much wonder the muck and concoctions she cooks — no sort of a cook, that's why he doesn't go there; no, George lives and dies here." Then, later, "Sitting in my house, eating my food, fiddling with my wireless, making his disgusting noises. Talking about his inside, I don't want to be told about what's going on in his inside — I can hear! His quack medicines, his lurid talk of murder and scandals, I've put up with it all these years, but there is a limit. Making himself a laughing stock, riding that tricycle about the place — that tricycle, that's another of his fads — I wish he had it in him, the cratur! And his language is worse than ever, I was never brought up to hear such words as belly and bum. If my poor Mother knew I was hearing such talk she'd turn in her grave and my Father would horsewhip him. And to have to sit and listen to that great stomach of his rumbling for hours on end — it's all that trish-trash he keeps swallowing, it's having a war in there. Thank goodness I never had any daughters to have to suffer his vulgar ways. The things he says to people! Going up to decent respectable women and asking if they've lost their drawers, and then yesterday talking about men putting their hands up — oh! oh!. And to crown it all, this black market business he's mixed up in. And now my only sister refuses to come this summer — I know what it is, she won't face the brute! I'm warning you, he's driving me out of my mind!"

"I think I can hear Sandy on the wireless, Ethel. You'll miss him if you stop here talking. You'd better get off in the other room," said Father.

Chapter 16

HARVEST FESTIVAL

UNCLE and I were about to have tea, the cold fat bacon and a loaf of bread were on the table. Uncle got plates from the Welsh Dresser, and the bone-handled knives and forks, that had worn thin and sharp from countless years of use. I lifted the heavy iron kettle from the range to pour the boiling water into the blue enamel teapot.

"Uncle, there's something rolling about in the kettle."

"Oh, that's that egg."

"Egg?"

"Yes, I felt a bit peckish after dinner, so I popped an egg in the kettle to boil, then the Vicar called and I forgot all about it."

We ate our tea. I longed to know why the Vicar had called, but Uncle was reading the evening paper. When we were washed up, Uncle said, "I want you to give me a hand to decorate the church tomorrow."

"Decorate the church?"

"Yes, that's what the Vicar came about. George, he said, as our horticultural expert it would be nice if you'd decorate a window in the church for Harvest Festival. Vicar, I said, you couldn't have come to a better man, I said. Me and my nephew, we'll do it tomorrow, I said. He was as pleased as punch, 'cos of course he knew we'd make a first class job of it. You can depend on it, I said, and, he said, I know I can depend on you. The Vicar's a real good sort of chap, different to some of them you do read about."

The next day, we loaded two wheelbarrows up with vegetables and fruit, potatoes, onions, carrots, cabbage, beetroot, tomatoes, a pumpkin, Bramley apples, russet apples, custard marrows, Welsh marrows and two huge green and white vegetable marrows. Honesty (or Old Man's Beard) was placed on top of each barrow, rather like garnishing.

We trundled the wheelbarrows down the village street and when we reached The White Lion, Uncle popped in for a quick one while I remained outside guarding the barrows. Uncle brought me out a glass of fizzy lemonade.

As we continued down the village Dr. Higgins was just coming out of the surgery. "Hullo, George," he said. "You came to see me about that cough a couple of days ago."

"Aye, and chunt any better neither," grumbled Uncle.

"Well, put that bloody pipe out, then."

We pushed our barrows on towards the church. "'Pon my soul," said Uncle George, "that's no way for a doctor to talk."

We left the barrows in the porch and carefully carried the produce in to the church. There was enough stuff to do three windows and Uncle George took great pains over it, arranging and rearranging it all several times, stepping back to view the effect and then walking round to all parts of the church to see the effect from different angles. At last he was satisfied. I must say the windows looked well – I never realised Uncle was so artistic.

Just as we were about to leave, the Vicar came in. He was extremely pleased, "Well, well," he said, "that's magnificent, truly magnificent."

"I told you we'd make a capital job of it, Vicar," said Uncle.

"You have indeed, you have indeed," said the Vicar. "I heartily congratulate the two of you. And those splendid vegetables, so different from my poor specimens."

"You'd be able to grow better stuff if you paid more attention to my lectures, Vicar," said Uncle George. "I've seen you sat there before now with your eyes shut." "Oh, I do hope you didn't think I'd nodded off, the fact is I concentrate better with my eyes shut."

Mr. and Mrs. Palmer came into the Church, their arms laden with

116

vegetables and fruit.

"Oh! Oh Vicar!" squeaked Mrs. Palmer. "That's our window, who's done our window?"

The Vicar answered, "George here has done it, hasn't he done it beautifully?"

"But that's our window," chirped Mr. Palmer. "We always do that window."

"Never mind, you do the one next to it," said the Vicar.

"Oh no," squawked Mrs. Palmer, "If we can't do our window we won't do anything." And outside they rushed. We watched from the porch as they threw apples, potatoes and a marrow down on the church path and hurled carrots and a cabbage at tombstones.

"Twere some poorish old stuff anyhow," commented Uncle George. "That old mother Palmer always were a nasty, ill-tempered, chopsy old baggage."

Chapter 17

UNCLE GEORGE GOES TO TOWN

"WHERE'S Owen, wherever's the fellow got to? He promised me faithfully he'd be back here early. Why can't the fellow be on time? Hark! Hark! Can you hear him a-coming? 'Pon my soul, it's too bad of the fellow. When he does come, I'll give him a piece of my mind."

It was an early morning in October. There had been a sharp frost and Uncle George's breath was clearly visible, and as he fretted and fumed and paced angrily up and down the road, he really did look as if he was breathing fire, and, in a sense, he was. We were waiting for Owen Tishworth to come with his lorry and take the weaner pigs to market.

"If Owen ain't here in two seconds, I'll cuss him up hill and down dale when he does come."

Uncle went back to the pigs and gave them a little more dry meal, 'to pack'm out a bit.' I heard the sound of a lorry getting nearer, "Hark! Hark! Is that a lorry I hear?" asked Uncle. Owen drove up the road in his lorry; Uncle George ran out in the road to meet him; I followed.

"Mornin' George, sharp 'un last night, more running noses this morning than —" Owen Tishworth said, leaning out of the window with a cheery grin on his sharp featured face, his big black hat, as usual, looking as if it would fall down over his ears and cover his bristly face.

"Good morning, Owen," said Uncle, his bonhomie in odd contrast to the threats he'd been issuing earlier.

"Nice bunch of pigs, George" said Owen, when he'd backed his lorry up to the sty, "A very nice bunch of pigs."

"Damn good pigs, Owen, sorry I've got to part with 'em, but I haven't the food to run 'em on. They should top the market, shouldn't they?"

"I'll eat my hat if they don't, George."

"I should fry him."

"Eh, what's that you said, George?"

"I said I should fry your hat if I was you, Owen, he ought to sizzle well with all that grease on him."

Owen and I held some sheets of corrugated iron to guide the pigs, while Uncle George drove them out of the sty and up the tailboard of the lorry. When the pigs were safely penned inside the lorry Uncle gave a bolten of straw to Owen.

"Make sure you put 'em in a good place, Owen, and put 'em comfortable with this straw so's they can snuggle down and look nice, but not too much or it'll make 'em look small," instructed Uncle.

"We'll find a good place for 'em." Owen always referred to himself as 'we'.

"Put 'em comfortable, Owen."

"We'll put 'em comfortable, never you fear."

"Book 'em in and tell the auctioneer I'll be in."

"Don't you worry none."

"Begod, the auctioneer'll say that's some masters of pigs, Owen."

"They'm a nice bunch of pigs, a wonderful nice bunch of pigs."

"Drive steady with 'em, mind how you go."

"We'll do that."

"Ah well, mind how you go round sharp corners, and put 'em comfortable. Tell anybody you see that I've got a bunch of pigs in today."

"Ah, ah, we'll do that," answered Owen.

"Well then," said Uncle, suddenly impatient, "for God's sake get a move on, man, and get them pigs in to market instead of standing there blethering."

Half an hour later Uncle and I set off for market. His car was making a terrible noise.

"Me cirencester's gone," he bellowed in explanation.

As we went up a hill Uncle George leaned forward and going downhill he leaned backwards. All the way to market he gave a running commentary on other people's farming, interspersed with scathing remarks about other drivers on the road. "Rajah rhubarb, there's some bloody fools about this morning. Look, look, see what that muntle's just been and done? If I hadn't been quick there'd have

119

been an accident." Occasionally he wound the window down and shook a fist at some offender.

After parking the car we went to market and found his pen of pigs. Uncle George sat on the rails of his pen, and every time a farmer stopped to look at the pigs, Uncle would inform him, "A grand bunch of pigs, they'll do well. I bred 'em myself and I guarantee 'em absolutely. If you buy 'em you'll never regret it, I assure you." And if a few minutes elapsed without anyone stopping to look at them, Uncle George would buttonhole somebody and say, "I say, I say, are you looking for a bunch of weaners? There's a grand lot over there, got coats as slick as oonts, as soon as I saw 'em, I thought, there's a grand bunch of pigs, if ever I saw some good doers, this is them. They'll do some lucky chap a bit of good, I'll warrant."

While the auctioneer was selling them, Uncle George kept slipping in a bid. In an aside to me he whispered, "Just helping 'em on a bit." When they were sold Uncle George expressed partial satisfaction. They should, he said, have made a bit more, grand pigs like that were 'chup' at any price.

We saw Alfred Tucker, the butcher. "I came up by train," he said. "I don't know why I come, force of habit I suppose. I can't buy what I like nowadays, I've got to have what they send me. Not like the old days, when the best beasts in the market came into the ring to be sold and the auctioneer cried, 'Here's some beasts to suit Alfred Tucker; bid up, gentlemen, bid up, you'll have made your reputation if you can buy 'em over the head of Alfred Tucker.' Ah, it's not like that today, not like the days when only the very, very best were good enough for Alfred Tucker." Mr. Tucker walked sadly off, shaking his head, his gait but a poor shadow of his former swagger.

"He's a-charging the earth for under the counter venison. I reckon Reuben have got something to do with that, old Reuben's got as close as an oyster lately — he's doin' his eye good at summat," said Uncle.

Just then, a tall farmer in breeches and leggings came up and spoke to Uncle. "I've just sold my beans to the merchant. I said to one of my chaps when we threshed 'em, no beast will ever pay to eat them at £2 a bag, so I've sold 'em."

Uncle made some remarks about the weather and farm prices. The farmer replied, "The men are doing better than us, high wages, no worries or responsibilities — when they knock off at night they're finished for the day — not like me. And if it's raining they put my sacks over their shoulders and never bring 'em back; at a tanner a time, they're on to a good thing. But can't say a word to them now, they're that independent — some of 'em are joining the Farm Labourers Union, but you've got to keep your mouth shut. They oughtn't to be allowed to join a union, and I said so at the Farmers Union meeting the other night. Funny times we live in. Even the police, you don't know where you are with them nowadays, they treat a gentleman in just the same way as they do a working man, I suppose it's all right, but it's a damn funny way of going on."

And with that he strode off. "Worth pots of money," said Uncle, "but always moaning. He begrudges to see anybody else make a bob."

Several merchants had little wooden huts in the market. Uncle stopped at one and said to the man inside, "Missed you when you called last week. It was a wet morning and I went down to The Lion. Send my pig food on as soon as you can, will you?" Uncle started nodding his head at the man and winking. "Squeeze out an extra bag or two if you can."

We walked on through the market, stopping occasionally while Uncle spoke to some acquaintance. Eventually we reached the market entrance and walked out into the street. "Remind me to go to the ironmongers to get some pig rings, your Father hasn't got any and he don't know when he'll get any more. But first we'll go in here and have some fish and chips. The Radio Doctor says fish and chips are first class grub."

All the time we were eating, Uncle kept muttering "First class grub." When we had finished we walked towards the ironmongers.

As we were walking along the street, I noticed that Uncle George's left boot had a hole in it as big as a shilling, just about where his little toe was. "Course I know I got a hole there, I made it. Really boy, you ain't as bright as you were, it's to ease my bunion. I went down to the Doctor's the other night and after he'd had a look at it, he said, 'Let's see the other foot,' and I told'n there was no need to do that as thic'n was all right, but he insisted, some doctors get these fads you know. Now." Uncle George stopped walking and bent down and said confidentially, "if I'd a'known he was going to do a trick like that, I'd a washed both my feet."

By now we had reached the ironmongers. Uncle George suddenly stopped short and waved his stick at the window of the shop,

"Begod, just look there, boy." I looked and inside the window were a young man and woman sitting on a garden seat with their arms round each other. Uncle George stared at them for a moment or two and muttered, "Rajah Rhubarb." I gazed at them, fascinated, until Uncle crooked the handle of his stick round my arm and pulled me towards the shop door. We walked into the shop and Uncle asked the woman behind the counter for some pig rings. She nodded at us in a dreamy way; she was middle aged, had wispy grey hair, steel rimmed spectacles and sunken cheeks and mouth. She left us and then returned a few minutes after to say, "I'm sorry, but I've forgotten what you asked me for."

"I asked for pig rings, the sort you put in with a pliers," said Uncle.

"I'm awfully sorry, we haven't any pliers."

"I don't want pliers, only a box of pig rings."

"Oh I see, you just want the pig rings."

"Yes, just the rings."

"We've got the rings, that I do know because I saw them only this morning — no, no, I'm wrong, it was yesterday morning or — let me see, was it yesterday afternoon, yes, yes, it was yesterday afternoon I do believe."

"It'll be tomorrow morning afore any of us'll see 'em at this rate, missis," said Uncle.

"Now, now, Sir, you'll get me flustered and when I'm flustered I can't think at all and you'll never get your pig rings."

"Well, just keep calm, missis, and try to think where you d'keep 'em."

"In one of those drawers behind me, Sir, but I just can't recollect which one now, I'm that flustered."

"Well, try that one there," said Uncle leaning across the counter and pointing with stick, "that do look a likely un to me."

"All right, I'll look in that one, but I'm sure there's screws in there," she said and opened the drawer.

"There, there look, what did I tell you?" she said holding up a box of screws. "It's screws, I told you it was screws in there."

"Try the next un then," grunted Uncle.

She opened the next one and produced a set of false teeth.

"Look, look." She sounded overjoyed and held the teeth aloft. "There's my teeth."

"Dammit all, woman, I don't want yur tith, I want some pig rings."

"But don't you see, I took them out 'cos they were pinching this morning, and I'd forgotten where I put them, and couldn't eat my dinner," she replied.

"Now look here, my woman —." But just then the owner of the shop came in and started shouting, "Get those two fools out of that window, they're supposed to be serving customers not canoodling in the window on a garden seat. Oh, the staff I have to put up with these days, whatever will people think this shop is coming to! And that's the last garden seat, there won't be any more until after the war."

He rushed off to admonish the canoodlers who were being called from the window by the woman who had so recently found her teeth.

"Right, sir," she said to Uncle George, "I'll have the pig rings for you in a jiffy now. I can concentrate now I've got my teeth."

When we were out in the street Uncle George said to me, "Damn my rags, boy, there's some funny people about."

*　　*　　*　　*

"I want you to meet Miss Tingle," said Uncle George, leading me into a sweets and tobacco shop. An elderly lady with a thick scarf wound several times round her neck and a knitted hat on her head greeted Uncle, "Your usual, Sir?"

"Yes please, Miss Tingle, and something for my nephew," said Uncle.

"So this is your nephew, is it?"

"Yes, Miss Tingle, this is my nephew."

"I've heard a lot about you from your Uncle," she said.

"He'd like a few sweets, please."

"Sweets are very scarce, but I think I could find some for your nephew."

"That's what I told him. Sweets are getting scarce, I said, but Miss Tingle will find some for you."

"Shouldn't be surprised if they don't ration them," said Miss Tingle.

"I'll bring you a few nice vegetables the next time I come to market, Miss Tingle," said Uncle George.

"That's very good of you, Sir."

Miss Tingle handed Uncle George the tobacco and sweets, and I noticed she was wearing mittens and had difficulty in handling the money. "I hope we don't have a cold winter like last year," she said. "I don't know how I shall manage if we do, what with the blackout and the rationing and shortage of fuel — I do feel the cold, my blood's got thin."

"I hope we don't, Miss Tingle," said Uncle as we left the shop. I closed the door and Miss Tingle waved a mittened hand and gave me a wintry smile.

"Nice old lady" said Uncle George, thumping his walking stick down hard on the pavement, so hard that several passers-by stopped to stare at us.

"What are they gawping at?" asked Uncle. "Funny lot, townspeople, they'll stop and gawp at the slightest thing — and look at that lot over there." He waved his stick at a line of people on the other side of the road, waiting at a bus stop. "Look at their faces, from the looks on 'em you'd think as they was waiting to go into a concentration camp."

Thirty yards further down the street we came to a queue of people outside a shop. "Oho!" said Uncle, "what have we got here?" He tugged at the sleeve of a man at the end of the queue. "What's up then, what are you all waiting for?" he asked.

"I dunno," said the man, "I was just passing and saw the queue so I joined it."

"A damned peculiar thing to do, ain't it?" Uncle said.

"Oh, I dunno," replied the man, "but they've got something in the shop and I thought I might as well have it as anyone else."

"Well, all I hope is that you like it when you get it," said Uncle.

"Oh I dunno, it might be all gone afore I get there," said the man.

"You'll never know what you were queueing for then, will you?" said Uncle.

*　*　*　*

On the street corner we passed a blind man selling matches from a tray suspended from his neck.

"He's always there," said Uncle in a low voice. "Been there for years, he's not blind really, he's a detective watching people."

"Oh," I said, and mentally resolved not to be a detective after all, not if it meant standing on street corners for years. I'd keep pigs like Uncle instead, and grow fruit and vegetables. Perhaps I'd do a year or two at detecting first, and then if there was a baffling case Scotland Yard could always call me in. It would be rather like Sherlock Holmes being called from his bees. Not that I'd keep bees, I'd seen enough of that, old tin tray and all. I'd stick to pigs, poultry, fruit and vegetables, and cider. No doubt detectives would come and sit in my garden shed and drink cider while we discussed some particular knotty problem.

Uncle George interrupted my ruminations, "Over this crossing, boy." Halfway over the pedestrian crossing, Uncle George stopped and caught hold of my arm; he pointed with his stick to the square metal studs in the road and at the Belisha beacons on either side.

"Always make sure you cross the road at one of these crossings, 'cos if you get knocked down on one of these crossings you'll stand a better chance of getting some compen." He directed my attention to the studs and the beacons once again, and then seemed lost in thought.

We were beginning to hold the traffic up, Uncle and I standing there in the middle of the road, but Uncle seemed in no hurry to move. A couple of motorists sounded their horns and another shouted, "Are you going to stand there all day?" Uncle George waved his stick at them and stood his ground.

"Come on Uncle," I said.

"Oh all right," he replied, but he waved his stick at the impatient motorists again and told them, "We've got the right of way you know."

*　　*　　*　　*

When we were on the pavement he said, "We're going to see Mrs. Sackville now, at the wine shop just around the corner." We paused outside the shop and Uncle adjusted his hat and gave his coat a perfunctory flick, he blew his nose hard in a large red handkerchief, and then ordered me to open the door.

The shop was rather dark. On the shelves behind the counter were a few bottles, otherwise the place was empty. Uncle saw me looking at the bottles and chuckled, "They're fakes m'boy, there ain't much drink about now because of the war, but what stuff they've got they keep out at the back, out of sight y'know, for special customers." I inferred from the nods, winks and nose rubbing that Uncle was one of these favoured special customers for whom stuff was kept at the back.

"Anybody about, anybody about?" asked Uncle and rapped the counter with the handle of his stick. "Anybody about?" But no one came and Uncle rapped on the counter louder and shouted, "Anybody about?" He began to tap a bit of a tune with his stick on the counter and mutter, "Ho-hum, ho-hum, wonder where Mrs. Sackville is, anybody could rob the place if only there was something to rob, ho-hum, ho-hum." With his left hand he began to beat time, he appeared to be enjoying himself and smiled broadly at me and shook his head from side to side. A thin faced, middle aged woman came hurrying in, Uncle immediately stopped his performance and raised his hat decorously. "How do you do, Mrs. Sackville" he said, "and how's your health today? You were a bit middling the last time I saw you, Mrs. Sackville."

"I'm much better, thank you."

"I'm very glad to hear it. When I got back I said to my brother, Mrs. Sackville is out of sorts today, and he was quite worried about it. He said, it's not like Mrs. Sackville to be ill and I told him the very next time I was in town I'd make a special point of calling to see how you were, Mrs. Sackville, and he asked to be remembered to you. He said, remember me to Mrs. Sackville, won't you, George?"

"That was very kind of him."

"Both of us have known you since you were quite a small girl, Mrs. Sackville."

"And how is your brother keeping?"

"Oh, he's very well, of course Ethel, his wife, you know Ethel his wife, don't you Mrs. Sackville? She looks after him very well, she's a capital cook you know."

"Has he still got the shop?"

"Yes, but he's got a job to get stock these days. And how's your old Father, Mrs. Sackville? How's he keeping? I've known your Father since I was a bit of a boy-chap, Mrs. Sackville. I always thought a lot of your Father, Mrs. Sackville, always a great respect for your Father, but who didn't? A very highly respected man. How is your Father, Mrs. Sackville?"

"Fairly well, considering his age. I suppose we mustn't grumble, considering his age."

"I must tell my brother. This is my brother's boy I've got with me. I've brought him in to see my pigs sold and now we're going round the town doing a bit of business here and there — ah now, your Father, a wonderful old gentleman, oh, he'll be greatly missed when he goes on, Mrs. Sackville. There's not many about like him. Give him my best wishes, won't you? Yes, yes, he's a great age, a wonderful age and still fairly active. Oh he's a marvellous old gentleman, Mrs. Sackville."

Uncle moved a few paces from the counter. "I promised my brother I'd come to see how you are, Mrs. Sackville, and to tell you the truth I've had you on my mind since I last saw you, you didn't look at all well, Mrs. Sackville, but I'm glad to see you're looking better today. Quite a bloom on you today, I'm happy to say, more like the old Mrs. Sackville."

Uncle raised his hat and turned as if to go, and then he turned again and walked slowly back to the counter. "Oh, I almost forgot," he said and leant across the counter. "I was wondering," he lowered his voice and in scarcely more than a whisper asked, "if you've got a bottle of whisky lying about?"

"Sorry, I haven't a drop on the place, you had a bottle only last week, I'll try and let you have one in a fortnight's time."

Uncle pulled a long solemn face and clicked his tongue. "Oh dear, oh dear, and I've got a bit of a cold coming on. Y'know a man of my age, outside working day and night, and in all winds and weathers, needs a drop of something warm at night, Mrs. Sackville."

"I'm sorry. In a fortnight's time."

"Oh dear, Mrs. Sackville, I shan't be in a fortnight's time. I was thinking of coming in next week and bringing you in a few eggs."

"I'll try and have a bottle for you next week."

"Oh, that's very good of you, Mrs. Sackville, very good indeed, and I'll bring you some eggs — but," a long pause and much furrowing of his brow, "if I can't get something for this cold, I can't promise to be here — and if I'm laid up — I suffer badly with my chest y'know, Mrs. Sackville. It's a wonder how I keep going, out in all winds and weathers, all hours of the day and night. If I'm laid up, goodness knows what'll happen. All the stock I've got to see to — oh, I dare not think about it — then I was going to kill a pig shortly — you like a bit of pigmeat don't you Mrs. Sackville? — I just don't know what'll become of it all."

"I've got a half bottle of rum I could let you have," said Mrs. Sackville.

"Oh, have you?" said Uncle George with great surprise. "How considerate of you, how exceedingly kind of you. Your Father was a considerate kindly man, we'll not see his like again when he passes on."

While Mrs. Sackville was absent, Uncle gave me a wink and looked very pleased. Mrs. Sackville returned with a bottle wrapped up in brown paper and handed it to Uncle, who carefully put it in the large pocket inside his coat. "Thank you very much, Mrs. Sackville, that's just what the doctor ordered, soak me bob if it ain't." He handed her a pound note and while she got his change he said in a voice as soft as the cooing of a pigeon, "Extremely thoughtful of you, Mrs. Sackville; you may have saved a poor, hardworking man's life, Mrs. Sackville."

She handed him some coins. "Thank you very much, Mrs. Sackville." Uncle raised his hat to her and on our way to the door he stopped to say, "I'll be in next week and," putting a forefinger to his nose, "I'll be bringing you a few eggs, Mrs. Sackville."

*　　*　　*　　*

Outside the wine shop Uncle George said, "I just want to slip down to the hospital; I've got an idea I might have to have an operation and I thought I'd pop in and see Spackman, the surgeon — he's very highly spoken of, I think he could manage my job all right — up and coming man y'know. If I don't get fixed up with him soon he'll be gone to Harley Street."

We walked along in silence. This was a terrible shock to me; I had no idea Uncle had anything seriously wrong with him. Only yesterday he'd been boasting that he'd never felt better in his life and he'd certainly seemed very well all day today. I felt very downcast. Poor old Uncle, all these years he'd been worrying and fretting about his health and we'd treated it as a bit of a joke. And all the time he'd really got something seriously wrong with him, the poor old boy, having to undergo an operation. I didn't think even Father knew he had to have an operation — poor old Father, he thought a lot of Uncle George, he'd be terribly upset about it, and as for Mother she'd be bound to get into a bit of a state — after all the nasty things she'd said about Uncle. As for me — my heart grew colder and heavier with every step we took.

I caught hold of Uncle's hand and looked up at his face — he didn't seem the least bit perturbed. There he was striding along, a serene look on his face. He saw a couple of people he knew on the other side of the street and waved his stick to them. Dear Uncle George, brave Uncle George, I could only hope that everything would be all right and that if ever the day came for me to have an operation, that I should be half as brave as Uncle George.

We entered the hospital, a grim forbidding place. I gripped his hand tighter. Uncle George spoke to the receptionist, "I want to see Mr. Spackman, the surgeon, please."

"Have you an appointment, sir?" she asked.

"That's what I've come about. I want him to do a little job for me."

"Has your Doctor made an appointment?" she asked.

"Of course he hasn't."

"Have you got a letter from your Doctor?"

"Why should I have a letter from my Doctor?"

"To give to Mr. Spackman."

"I'm not a postman, young lady — I'm a farmer, and I want Mr. Spackman to operate on me."

"Have you seen your Doctor about it?"

"It's no good to see him, he doesn't understand this sort of thing — this is a job for a surgeon."

"I'm sorry, sir, you must see your own doctor first."

"A complete waste of time young woman, just tell me where Mr. Spackman is and I'll pop and have a word with him now I'm here — won't take a few minutes."

"I'm sorry, Mr. Spackman's not here to-day."

"Has he gone up to London to see about a place in Harley Street?" asked Uncle George.

"No, no, sir, he doesn't come in on Tuesdays, that's all."

"Thank the Lord for that — for a minute I thought I'd left it too late — has he got any plans for going to Harley Street, d'you know?"

"I have no idea what Mr. Spackman's plans are, sir," the receptionist said firmly. "You go and see your doctor and he'll see to it all. Now you must excuse me, I've got a lot of work to do."

Out in the street Uncle George said, "Damn my rags — I've never heard the like of it, what are things coming to? That chit of a girl in there telling me to see my own doctor — what the hell does he know about a complaint like mine?"

*   *   *   *

We made our way back to where the car was parked, stopping at a chemist's shop. "Right," said Uncle George, "in here."

"Good afternoon, sir," said the white coated chemist, a small bespectacled man with a shining bald head who evidently knew Uncle well. "What can I get for you?"

Uncle unbuttoned his jacket and fished in his waistcoat pocket and eventually produced a newspaper cutting which he showed to the chemist. "Have you got any of this here stuff?" said Uncle. The chemist nodded. "Is it any good on?" asked Uncle. "The paper do speak very well of it."

"It's a new preparation, and I haven't heard any reports about it yet," said the chemist.

"Give me three large packets," said Uncle.

"Yes, sir, will there be anything else today, sir?"

"Ah, — well, — now let me see — a large box of charcoal tablets and — um — a packet of senna pods and um, some Friars Balsam and some liver pills and, well, I mightn't be in for a bit so you'd better let me have a tin of my usual salts and some corn plasters. Oh, I almost forgot, some Beechams Powders and some iodine and aspirin — at this time of the year you can't be too well stocked up."

"Quite right sir, thank you sir — I often think if more people were like you and took good care of themselves, there wouldn't be the illness about and doctors wouldn't be rushed off their feet."

"Some of the doctors aren't much bottle neither," said Uncle grimly. "Oh, and I'll have one of them tins of Zubes."

The chemist packed the lot up and Uncle paid him. Out in the street again Uncle muttered to himself, "Perhaps that new stuff'll do the trick," and to me, "A busy hardworking man like me can't afford to be messed about by that hospital's fiddle-assing nonsense."

*   *   *   *

We turned down a side street. "We must go to Mr. Benjamin, I want to see about my grandmother," said Uncle George. Mr. Benjamin, I discovered, was a watch and clock repairer. His shop was down a narrow street, and we opened a door which had dirty green paint blistered and peeling off it, the doorbell rang and we found ourselves in a very small room. A querulous little man came in from somewhere behind the counter and stood blinking at us. "I haven't any clocks or watches for sale," he announced.

"I've come about a repair," said Uncle.

"I can't take any more repairs, I'm right full up," he answered.

"I've come about my grandmother, which you've already got."

"Why didn't you say so in the first place?"

"You never gave me much of a chance," said Uncle George.

"When did you bring it in?" he asked.

"About three years ago."

"Well, I don't expect it's done yet, these things take time."

"You've taken yours and mine."

"You haven't come here to complain, have you?" he asked anxiously.

"No, no, only to enquire."

"I'm glad of that, I can't stand folks who complain and I can't take any interest in their work either."

"How's the old girl getting on, then?"

"Old Girl? What old girl and how should I know how she is?" Mr. Benjamin asked, looking puzzled.

"My grandmother clock I mean," explained Uncle.

"Why didn't you say that in the first place? You sure you haven't come to complain?"

Uncle shook his head.

"If you'll just wait a minute, I'll go down to the cellar and see."

He returned about five minutes later, looking very distressed, and said, "Oh dear-oh, there's so many clocks down there, I don't know which is yours. It's hardly reasonable of you, sir, to walk in here and expect me to know which is your clock. You'd better come down with me and identify it."

Mr. Benjamin led the way, and after we were down four or five steps he stopped and looked at us. "Be careful, the steps are very steep."

"It's dark down here," said Uncle.

"Of course it is," snapped Mr. Benjamin. "There are no windows, surely you don't expect windows in a cellar?" Uncle told him he didn't expect to find windows in a cellar, and Mr. Benjamin replied, "Then it was rather a silly thing to say, wasn't it?"

"I meant, how are we going to see?" said Uncle.

"That isn't what you said, now is it, sir?" He gave a sniff and added, "If you'd said what you meant I should have told you that I have a candle down there."

"Is a cellar a good place to keep clocks, Mr. Benjamin?" asked Uncle.

"No, it's too damp really, but I brought them down here because of the war. My Father brought clocks down here in the last war and nobody complained. Are you sure you're not complaining?"

Uncle George assured him he wasn't complaining.

"Absolutely sure?" asked Mr. Benjamin.

"Absolutely."

"Because some people are never sure whether they're complaining or not, and complaining upsets me. Mrs. Benjamin knows, she can tell in a minute. As soon as I get home at night she says, Jacob, you're upset, somebody's been complaining."

The candle was lit and we saw the cellar was full of clocks, grandfathers and grandmothers, marble clocks, French carriage clocks, clocks of all shapes and sizes. Mr. Benjamin placed his hands on his stomach and said wistfully, "Such a lot of clocks, some of them I've had for a long time, some of them belong to me and belonged to my father and his father. The others belong to people who've brought them to me to repair, some of them have been here for a long time, too. Some people bring them here and forget about them, or go away and die. I think some bring them here to have a good home, to somebody who'll look after them and be kind to them. You can get very attached to a clock, you know. I keep all my favourite ones at home, the very favourites in our bedroom; I like to hear the sound of their ticking as I lie in bed. Mrs. Benjamin is very fond of clocks, too, such a wonderful thing for a man and wife to be fond of the same things, you know."

While Mr. Benjamin had been talking, Uncle had been looking for his clock and at last he found it. "Ah, here's my grandmother," Uncle said and patted the clock.

"Aha, sir, I can see you're fond of your clock. When I get home tonight Mrs. Benjamin will know in a minute. Jacob, she'll say, you've had somebody in today who's fond of his clock."

"I am fond of her, Mr. Benjamin. She belonged to my mother."

"Aha, sir, you needn't tell me, I know. I can see you're a man after my own heart. Oh! I can hardly wait to get home to tell Mrs. Benjamin, sir."

"How long will it be before she's put right?" asked Uncle.

"Well, in your case, I'll make an exception. I'll put a ticket on it. Urgent, I'll write on it, and I'll have it ready for you in four months."

"Do you like eggs, Mr. Benjamin?"

"I do, sir, and Mrs. Benjamin does, but we don't often get the chance of any now."

"I could bring you some in a month's time."

"Oh, could you, sir? And I think I could have your clock ready for you at the same time, sir."

"Beautiful big brown eggs."

"Beautiful brown eggs! Oh, when I get home tonight I'll tell Mrs. Benjamin that the gentleman who is so fond of his clock is bringing us some beautiful brown eggs."

"And a marrow."

"Ah, marrow too? Mrs. Benjamin stuffs them, we love stuffed marrow. It is very kind of you, sir."

"Two marrows, if you like, and some eggs, Mr. Benjamin."

"You are very kind, sir, very kind indeed."

"See you in a month's time then, Mr. Benjamin," said Uncle George as we left the shop.

We walked back to the place near the market where the car was parked. The blind man was still at the street corner selling matches. "Do you really think he's a detective, Uncle?" I asked.

"Oh yes, he's a detective, but I'm not supposed to know, so keep mum about it, it'd be no bottle if every Tom, Dick and Harry knew he was a detective watching them."

"Surely he has a job to watch people through those dark glasses?"

"Oh, I expect that's a trick of the trade."

We reached the car and Uncle was just about to get in to it, "Rajah rhubarb!" he exclaimed. "I damn near forgot! I must get some pig powders and some Karswood's poultry spice. For the life of me I can't fathom why your Father don't stock 'em. The times I've told him there's a big demand for pig powders and poultry spice."

We went to the corn chandler's near the market. The market was over now, a few lorries were there, still being loaded with stock, and some farmers were standing about in little groups, with, Uncle George said, "Their guts bustin' with beer."

We carried the cartons of pig powders, the large yellow packet of Karswood's poultry spice, and the bag of Glauber's salts back to the car.

"Quite a day," said Uncle George when we were almost home.

Chapter 18

THE SHOOTING AFFAIR

WE never heard another word about the operation, so that 'new preparation' must have 'done the trick'.

But Uncle George was still grumbling because Father didn't stock pig powders and poultry spice when he came to get his broad bean seeds a few days later. Father sold seeds, garden fertilisers such as blood and bone meal, and other garden sundries; dairy equipment for the local farmers, milking stools, buckets and strainers and tools at his shop, besides hardware.

"Pig powders, worming powders, poultry spice and grit, globber salts, epsom's, sulphur, rock salt, you oughta sell 'em all," he told Father. "There's a call for 'em, there's money in 'em and if you don't stock 'em, Pemberthy will. I see he's started selling garden cloches. He's had one over you on that job, you ought to've been selling them, not him. A shrewd business man, Pemberthy."

"He's a fly one," said Father.

"Ah, and you gotta be, in business. When I had the bakery business I was as keen as mustard. I was about, I was about."

"Yes, you were about all right, all hours of the day and night, never finished work and never really started. People got sick to death of you bumbling about at all hours, waking them up with your wretched bread, that's those who were lucky enough to be included on a delivery round." This came from Mother who'd just come into the shop.

"There's no need to go at our George like that, Ethel," said

Father. "He was only trying to be helpful, like he always is."

"Ah, using you to stock the stuff that he only wants to buy in drib drabs. It's a wonder he doesn't ask you to stock that stuff he fakes his cider up with."

*   *   *   *

The following afternoon when I called on Uncle George, I couldn't find him anywhere outside. He wasn't in the garden and the pigs were squealing for their food, there was no sign of him in the orchard, and the hens all came running round me looking for their corn. I looked in the poultry houses and saw that the eggs had not been collected, so I went back into the garden and looked in the garden shed. I thought perhaps he'd nodded off in there. The back door of the house was open, so I went in. I stood in the kitchen and heard a low moaning coming from the parlour.

Uncle George rarely, if ever, used the parlour. The room smelt musty and mousey; the chrysanthemum-patterned wallpaper was stained with damp, and small pieces of newspaper were pasted over it in several places. Uncle George was troubled by mice and the newspaper on the walls, like the tin nailed to the skirting, was covering up the mouse holes. Drab, cracked linoleum covered the floor, and over by the fireplace (never used) that was filled with fir cones, was a rag rug. Over the fireplace hung the 'Relief of Mafeking' and on the back of the door, suspended on a piece of binder twine threaded through one corner, hung a curled up copy of Old Moore's Almanack.

A great number of Sexton Blake stories, Culpeper's Herbal, The Country Gentleman's catalogue, and a Home Doctor were stuffed haphazardly into a rickety old bookcase. On the mantelpiece was a bust of Sexton Blake about seven inches high, and on either side of this stood a huge black vase embossed with vivid pink roses and filled with plumes of dried pampas grass which were covered in dust. A stiff collar and tie hung on the mirrored back of the chiffonier on which were scattered several studs and buttons and a pile of seed catalogues. In the corner was a very old, brown, worm-eaten piano and stool. The only other furnishings were an old horsehair sofa and two matching chairs, and two floor length curtains of red fringed chenille which were rotten with age and would have fallen to pieces if anybody had attempted to draw them.

* * * *

Uncle George lay face downwards on the sofa, moaning. When he realised that I was in the room, the moaning increased. "Oooooh . . ., I'm in agony, oooooooh . . ."

"Are you hurt, Uncle?"

"Oooooooh . . . – damn it all boy, would I be lying here like this and groaning if I weren't? Rajah rhubarb! I'm all but done for. Oh-oh-oh, oooooh . . ., that you should see your poor old Uncle in such a state. Oooh . . . that I should be cut short in me prime, oooooh . . ."

Uncle George stopped his groaning and turned on his side to look up at me. He let out a shriek and rolled back on to his stomach and continued to groan.

I offered to go and get the doctor as quickly as I could. Uncle stopped his moaning at once and jumped to his feet. "Don't you do that! I don't want to see that bloody doctor, it's all his doing. By God, if I don't get some compen from the murderer I'll get him struck off the register. I don't want to see a bloody doctor as long as I live, a plague on doctors – don't you ever mention doctor to me again, a danger to the community. I'll have him in court, that I will, oooooh . . ., it's teart m'boy. Ooooooh . . ., that I should have to suffer like this, oooooh . . ., what is the world coming to? A law abiding man ain't safe in his own garden now, ooooh . . . Fetch the whisky, boy!"

After I'd poured him some whisky, I ventured to ask what was the matter. "The matter, boy? I've been shot! I've been shot, shot in the arse by that muntle Higgins, the murderous idiot!" He paused and drank his whisky, then went on, "There I was, out there in the garden, planting my broad beans, and rajah rhubarb! Bang! I was shot

136

in the arse, my poor backside blown to flickets. Down I go like Aunt Sally, down I go like a ninepin — wallop! I thought I was a jud 'un. Up prances Higgins, the murderer, and says 'Oh, George, I'm fraghtfully sorry, I appear to have peppered you in the bum.' Peppered me in the bum indeed! The bugger had blasted me backside to kingdom come!"

Uncle George stopped for a minute and screwed his face in agony. I was too worried at the time, but, on recollection, I think it was the finest performance he had ever given of grotesque faces. Then he continued, "There I lay, on the cold damp earth, my broad bean patch being fertilised by my own blood, beans I should never live to eat. I could feel all the life ebbin' out of me, I writhed in mortal agony. All me past life flashed before me and I could just dimly hear that murderous bloody Higgins saying as calm as you like, 'Come on, my man, get on your feet and I'll help you into the house. There's no need for you to worry,' he says, 'I'll soon get the shot out and I won't charge you'. And I thought, no, but I'll charge you with bloody murder. Then he has the cheek to say, 'I wasn't shooting at you, George, I was shooting at rabbits'. That proves the bugger's mad, I ask you, could you mistake me for a rabbit?

"After I'd staggered into the house, and God knows how I managed it, a lesser man would have died on the way, he says, 'Now just lie on that sofa until I get back, and for heaven's sake, stop that dreadful caterwauling, there's no need for you to worry.'

"After he'd gone, I lay in agony and thought, he's hopped it and left me to die. Another unsolved murder, that's what I'll be, just like the Torso mystery. I could just see the headlines in next Sunday's *News of the World*, UNSOLVED MURDER OF WELL KNOWN COUNTY MAN, or POPULAR YEOMAN DONE TO DEATH, or MURDER MOST FOUL OF DISTINGUISHED LAND OWNER, and of all the people from miles around who'd come to my funeral and the detectives from Scotland Yard mingling with 'em."

Uncle George, who looked a great deal better by this time, puffed out his cheeks and ordered me to pour out a 'stiffish 'un'. "I reckon the 'tecs'd 'ave got the bloodhounds out, scouring the countryside," he muttered.

"But that dastardly Higgins hadn't realised the manner of man I was." Uncle looked cunning and produced a slip of paper which he handed to me. I looked at the paper which said, "Dr. Bloody Higgins did me in. He is a dangerous lunatic, arrest him at once before he kills the whole village." Uncle George said, "I put it in me weskit pocket and thought, that'll stop his little game; then I lay down on the sofa and made my peace with my Maker. I was quite calm at the end."

I pointed out, tactfully I hope, to Uncle George that he was still alive.

"Course I be, boy, 'pon my soul, I sometimes think you be losin' yer wits. Do you think I should be standing here talking to you if I were a jud 'un? My constitution saved me — and that Dr. Higgins came back — that was a shock, I'll admit — and pulled the shot out, and rajah rhubarb, that hurt more'n 'em goin' in. Mind, I never made a murmur, I wasn't goin' to give him the satisfaction of hearin' me howl, and, 'There,' he said, 'that's all over. No need to make a fuss, I'm not charging you."

I said that I didn't think that Dr. Higgins was really the murderous sort.

"Doctors not murderous! You can never tell, just look at that Crippen!"

Uncle George had another 'stiffish 'un' and opened his eyes as wide as he could, "Fuss! He'll find there'll be fuss, if I don't get some compen!"

I went out and fed the pigs and fowls and collected the eggs. When I got back, Uncle George was having yet another 'stiffish 'un'. He looked more his old self now and I was no longer worried, so I went home after promising to come again in the morning to see to the animals.

Before going to school next morning, I went to feed the stock for Uncle. I would've liked to stay home from school, but I'd got in enough trouble about the day I had off to go to market. Uncle's bedroom curtains were still drawn, so I didn't disturb him after his terrible experience the day before. I called on my way home in the afternoon and Uncle George seemed less angry with the doctor. I learned later that Doctor Higgins had been to see him and left a few gifts, together with the promise of further ones to follow. A beautiful big salmon, I gathered, would be coming as soon as the salmon fishing season opened.

"Agnes has been round to help out and has brought some cake and some fish, and Higgins will be calling later to see how I am. He's bringing a bottle of whisky. It seems I was a bit hasty yesterday, bit of an accident, you know. I always said that Higgins was a fairish doctor, shouldn't like to lose him by gettin' him struck off. And he's takin' an interest in me — give him his due — but rajah rhubarb, if he ever does such a thing again, I'll have him struck off."

We fed the pigs and poultry and Uncle Greorge took me to the scene of the crime. "There," he said and pointed his stick, "there, that's where I fell, you can still see the marks. If I'd have died the police would have taken plaster casts and there'd have been pictures in the *News of the World*."

I prepared tea in the kitchen, while Uncle George stood by the mantelpiece making grimaces in the mirror. "We could have had that fish that our Aggie brought, if the darnation cats hadn't stole it."

By the end of the next week, Uncle George had almost forgotten about the accident. I noticed several bottles of whisky on the chiffonier in the parlour, a brace of pheasants hanging in the pantry and a plentiful supply of tobacco stacked on the dresser in the kitchen. As we strolled out into the orchard to pick the Ribston Pippins he told me, "Higgins isn't a bad old stick. I've decided to bury the axe."

On Sunday, not a word was said about the affair — there was, as far as I can remember, a particularly shocking scandal in the *News of the World.* During Mr. Middleton's broadcast on gardening, Uncle George did a lot of cheek puffing and after the broadcast he said, "I believe he's failing. Did you notice what a job he had to breathe? It's all taboo. And he hasn't got quite the right approach." Again I noticed, but didn't understand, the gleam in Uncle George's eyes.

Mother brought the tea in after Mr. Middleton's talk and Uncle said, "Did you go to the Whist Drive on Friday, Ethel?"

"Yes, I did, and won the lady's first prize, a very nice jar of hand cream."

"But did Len Wilson put his hand on your knee, Ethel?"

"No, George, he didn't. But after you telling me about him, I mentioned it to Mrs. Gerrish and she said it's perfectly true he does do it, so I took particular notice. And I noticed that several of the women, especially the younger ones, would sit sideways, so that their backs were towards him, when they were at his table. If he as much as put his hand near me, I'd slap his face, the horrible disgusting wretch!"

Father said, "He's a damned bad bagger and no mistake."

"Did you hear about him offering Mrs. Elford a lift into town? He started his monkey capers with her, frightened the poor woman out of her wits, she told me so herself. If that Micah had anything about him, he'd give him a damned good hiding," said Uncle George. "You know that old fool's gone in for goatkeeping now? I thought the fish stink'd kill me, but be jiggered, them goats — the nannies ain't so bad, but that old billy, pooh — don't he forever whistle. Old Micah's a damned bad neighbour, y'know. I feel sorry for his wife, a nice little woman, far too good for that varmint."

"If you like to bring me your fat ration, George," Mother said, "not your butter of course, I'll make you some pies and cakes. I've already made my Christmas puddings and there'll be one for you, I know how fond you are of them."

Uncle George thanked her very much and I could see Father was delighted that Mother was so much nicer to Uncle these last few days. While Uncle and Father were talking about the war, Mother brought us some cake. Uncle George munched away in silence, apparently lost in thought, and suddenly murmured, almost inaudibly, "They'll have to replace him soon. The B.B.C.'ll be on the look out."

Chapter 19

THE BROADCAST

"IF George isn't here soon, he'll miss the Radio Doctor," said Mother. "And I've got his breakfast all ready. It'll be too bad if he doesn't turn up."

"He'll be here in a minute," said Father, sitting down to his breakfast.

"I hope so, I've done some toast for him, he's very partial to a bit of toast."

"You've got very fond of George all of a sudden, haven't you, Ethel?"

"Oh, he's not a bad sort really. I feel a bit sorry for him all alone in that house."

A few minutes later Uncle George arrived, and before he sat down at the table he handed Mother an envelope. "Thank you, George," she said, and furtively tucked it behind the clock on the mantelpiece.

"What's that then, Ethel?" asked Father. Father was supposed to be rather deaf and he often gave the impression of being vague and unobservant, but there was little that he missed; he was deaf and unobservant purely for his own convenience.

"Just a little secret between George and me," Mother answered evasively, and started pouring tea.

"Good job I'm not like Amos Bloxham, or there'd be hell-to-pop," grunted Father, but I could see that he was pleased that Mother was being so nice to Uncle George.

"Hush now," said Mother, "or George won't be able to hear the Radio Doctor."

As soon as he'd finished his breakfast, Uncle George said he must be off, he had a busy day ahead of him.

"Goodbye George, and thank you," Mother called after him.

"You two're too thick to last," said Father.

Mother quickly cleared the dishes; she seemed in a hurry. I got myself ready for school and Father went off to open the shop.

I was in the shop talking to Father, when mother came in and said, "I'll put your dinners in the oven, I'm catching the eleven-ten train into town."

"I had no idea you were going to town today, Ethel," said Father. "Whatever in the world are you canking there for?"

"I thought I'd go and get myself a new coat and frock for the winter."

"What about the dockets, only the other day you were complaining you hadn't any clothing dockets — well, I'll be damned — so that's what our George gave you in that envelope. So that's why you've been making such a fuss of poor old George. As you'd say yourself, 'a sprat to catch a mackerel'."

"I'll be back on the three-fifteen," said Mother, as she swiftly withdrew, her face rather red.

* * * *

Uncle George peered at me over the top of the spectacles he wore for writing. He was sitting at his kitchen table, a bottle of ink and a pad of ruled writing paper before him, and a pen in his hand. "Hullo, boy, I'm doing a spot of writing." He put his head on one side, puckered his face, and with his tongue between his lips, he continued with his writing.

I sat silently in the armchair until Uncle had finished the letter and sealed the envelope by licking the flap well, and then, placing the envelope on the table, thumped it hard several times.

"I've had a most unpleasant duty today," he said. "A most unpleasant duty. I've been down to the butcher and told him straight, 'Look here, Alfred,' I said, "What's the meaning of sending me all this cagmag?' I said. 'Here I am, producing some of the finest beef in all England and all I get to eat is cagmag. Chun't good enough,' I said. Poor old Alfred, he looked a bit taken aback. 'It ain't my fault, George,' he said. 'I've got to have what I'm allocated.' 'Well, it's a bloody scandal,' I told him; and he said, 'I'm very sorry about it, George, but there's nothing I can do about it.' 'Well,' I said, 'it's about time somebody did something about it.' And poor old Alfred said, 'Please don't blame me. If you want to complain write to Lord Woolton, he's the Minister of Food, not me, complain to him.'

142

'Ah,' I said, 'I'll do that, Alfred, because I wants to bloody complain right enough.' And that's what I've just been doing. I've told Lord Woolton, and I ain't minced me words neither."

Uncle drew the writing paper towards him and dipped his pen in the ink. "And now," he said sternly, "I'm going to write to Mr. Hudson, Minister of Agriculture. Huh! And what does he know about agriculture I'd like to know? — Soap, that's his business; well, just let him try his soft soap on me. I shall tell him that I'm struggling to keep the country's pig population a goin' and I need more pig food than I'm getting. Just you sit quiet, I won't be long."

There was nobody like Uncle George for putting a letter together. Father often said, he'd got a head on him like a lawyer. Uncle George was certainly finding it a problem getting enough food for the pigs and poultry. However, by helping other farmers with their threshing he managed to get some extra corn.

We were into December and Uncle's favourite Old Spot sow had recently farrowed. She had twelve piglets, all alive and well, but it meant that there were extra mouths to feed.

While Uncle wrote the letter, I read a *Sexton Blake*. A thump, thump, thump, told me the letter was finished and sealed in the envelope. "I told him straight, but I doubt if it'll do much good. All these politicians are the same, even the Speaker, I don't forget the way he behaved, neither."

He propped the two letters against a milk jug on the table, "Just pop those two in the box on your way home; I have stamped 'em." He turned towards me and noticed the book I was reading. "That's a good 'un. Old Sexton don't half get in a tight corner, but Tinker and Pedro get there in the nick of time. I wonder if old Pedro ever gets the worms — I had a dog once who had worms more'n a foot long, but I got some first class powders that soon shifted them."

We sampled the first of the season's beetroot wine.

"Here, boy, I knew I had something to tell you, I've been and taken a temporary job — just for a couple of weeks. They was a bit shorthanded down at the station, so I offered to help 'em out with the Christmas trees."

Our railway station enchanted me. It looked just like a railway station should, just like a child's model railway station. We had a signal box, waiting room, and a special ladies room, ticket office, parcels office, station master's and porters' rooms, two platforms joined by a lovely covered footbridge, and three lavatories labelled; LADIES, GENTLEMEN, and PORTERS. There were flower borders, which since the war had started, had been planted up with red pickling cabbage, on the station master's orders. This, he said, was because they looked as pretty as any flowers and were edible too.

There were also goods yards, and a pen for loading cattle, although most cattle were sent by road by this time, but many farmers had cattle food, basic slag and fertilizers arriving there in trucks. Three periods in the year brought great activity to the station when our local produce was despatched by the truck load, the local produce being: plums during August; sugar beet in late October and early November; and, in early December, the Christmas trees. These trees were grown by the thousand in plantations and were despatched to all parts of the country. Owen Tishworth was one of the hauliers who carted them from the woodlands to the station.

There was a camaraderie among the local women who travelled by rail. The same women always gathered at the station to catch the same train, on the same day of the week and they travelled to and from town together to do their shopping.

And now, Uncle George had taken a job at the station for a few hours each day.

On Sunday, Uncle George was able to tell us all the news of the station; how grand and important the station master thought himself, majestically strutting up and down the platform, twirling his waxed moustache when a train was about to arrive; who had sent parcels and where, who had received parcels and from whom, with shrewd guesses of what the parcels contained. How Len Wilson had come with a landgirl to collect cattle food. "We hid in the porters' room and watched, it were an eye opener — if I were you, Ethel, I'd stop away from them whist drives. If a fellow will carry on like he does in broad daylight, God Almighty knows what he'd do in the dark — 'tis no wonder that landgirls won't stop at Wilson's."

We were told who were Wednesday, Friday and Saturday women.

"I have," said Uncle George, "got that Christmas tree job well organised, I've got a system working like one o'clock. We do a bit of toast and bacon over the fire in the porters' room for dinner and warm a drop of cider. I've got it all real cosy down there, I shall be sorry when the job's over." It was abundantly clear that Uncle George was enjoying his temporary work.

The following Wednesday, Uncle George called at our house on his way home from the station. He was even more excited than the time when he told us about the spy being caught, or when he heard about the formation of the Marcle Watchers.

"The B.B.C. are coming tomorrow to the station, to do a recording about the Christmas trees. It's being broadcast over the whole country. This is my big chance." He looked very important and puffed out his chest as well as his cheeks, and once again I noticed the gleam in his eyes. But before we could ask him any questions, he said he must get his pigs fed and get straight off to bed. "I must have a good night's rest, tomorrow is my big day," and with that he was gone.

"I didn't like the looks of our George tonight," said Father.

*　　*　　*　　*

Uncle George called on his way to work next morning. He had his market boots on, the ones with the hole in the left foot. Underneath his khaki smock he was wearing his best suit. Instead of the usual spotted handkerchief round his neck, he wore a stiff collar and tie.

"What's all this dressing up for, George?" asked Mother.

"For my broadcast, of course," was his reply.

"But they'll only hear you, they won't see you, George."

"Oh ho, don't you be too sure about that, Ethel. I once read in the paper that the News Readers do wear evening dress, so that shows they ben't too sure."

"And what," asked Mother, "have you got in that frail?"

"Just a few bottles of parsnip wine to stop I from getting nervous. This is my big day and I ain't a taking no chances — why, I even had a bath last night, and cut me toe nails."

Most of the villagers went down to the station that afternoon to watch the broadcasters. I ought to have been at school, but Father said, "Let him go and see his Uncle broadcasting, Ethel." Mother demurred, but after dinner, when she'd changed into her new frock and coat, she relented, and said, "Very well, it seems a bit mean for me to be going and not to let him." I scampered off before she could change her mind and almost knocked Mrs. Gosworth over as I rushed through the shop doorway.

As I arrived Uncle George was just emerging from the porters' room, looking very red in the face. Had it been anyone other than Uncle George I'd have thought he was the worse for drink. Two B.B.C. vans were parked in the station yard, not far from the piles of Christmas trees. Two empty railway trucks were in the siding and a lorry load of Christmas trees was parked in the station approach. Several men and women from the B.B.C. were unloading equipment. The assembled villagers were surprised to see the normally staid railway porters actually rushing about, and after they had got over the initial shock of seeing the porters almost running, began to make ribald comments. All the railway staff were rushing about hither and thither, but none of them bustled about as much as Uncle George. The only person who remained calm was the stationmaster, who paced slowly up and down the platform, dignified and aloof.

Even Aunt Aggie had turned out. "It's getting nearer," she said to me confidentially. Most of Aunt Aggie's utterances were in this confidential tone. "What's getting nearer, Aunt Aggie?" I asked. "This broadcasting," she replied. "They'll be doing one at your Uncle Sam's factory soon I reckon. You know that 'Workers Playtime' programme? I'll be surprised if they don't ask your Uncle Sam to sing one of his comic songs, they'll like that better than that George Formy, and perhaps your Uncle Sam will be asked to go all over the country to cheer the war workers up. But I'm afraid the poor old fellow's health would never stand the strain of all the travelling. He never could stand travelling, riding on that bus to work makes him sea sick and causes him to do that dry heaving during the night; well, you know, nights and days, days and nights, we don't know which is which with this shifty work. It's got us all topsy-turvy. I go to bed when Sam does, it's the only way. Then there's all this messing about with clocks, why can't we just have God's time, that's what I want to know. It's never right to mess about with hours.

"And of course, you know your poor old Uncle Sam's suffering from that metal fatigue, suffering something chronic he is, that's all brought about by the war and working with metals in that factory; it saps it out of him; I've got him on iron tablets now, put some metal back into his system. It does seem to have brought a bit of colour into the old fellow's cheeks. It was your Uncle George who put him on to them and I'm forever thankful to him. Your Uncle George ought to have been a doctor, he's recommended some wonderful stuff to me at different times."

Amos Bloxham created a diversion when he came riding furiously down to the station on his bicycle; he looked most unsafe with his huge coat undone and flapping and brandishing his roadman shovel in his left hand.

Mrs. Gerrish had deserted her switchboard to come and see the broadcast. She was standing with Mother and Mrs. Gosworth who were soon joined by Mrs. Peabody wearing a hat of feathers and tulle.

Reuben Kimmins and Alfred Tucker arrived together and were soon joined by Bonnor Dawes and Micah Elford. Harry Paget came to collect the letters, and stopped to watch the proceedings and Zebrina pushing her baby daughter in the pram. We had recently heard that her husband had been awarded the D.F.C. Zebrina was very soon joined by her Father, Trophimus Ellicot. Trophimus was smoking a cigar and wearing a spotted bow tie, upon his head he had a homburg hat, his head poking forward and his shoulders bent.

Mrs. Fred Jenkins, sitting on a station hand trolley, was holding forth and laughing uproariously and in her excitement was leaning back as she laughed, legs in the air and giving us all a good view of her large pink bloomers.

Reuben catching sight of Uncle George shouted, "When they gonna start this yer broadcast then, George, we'm all a gettin' cold waitin' yur?" It was cold standing there on that bleak December afternoon, most of us were stamping our feet and rubbing our hands. Some of the younger children were beginning to tug at their mothers' arms and whimpering to be taken home. The women too, were beginning to lose interest in the broadcast, already they were talking about children, pregnancies, husbands, food rationing and so forth. The farmers and their workers were pulling watches out of their pockets and saying it would soon be milking time.

At last, at long last, the B.B.C. team were ready to begin. A man with a beard and dark spectacles held up his hand and asked for silence. The three-fifteen came in and after it had departed the man with the beard put his hand up again and asked for silence. Farmer Wilson drove up on his tractor and sat there puffing at his pipe and grinning vacantly, the tractor going full blast. The bearded man asked someone called Fred, to ask that yokel to take his confounded contraption away. Len Wilson had only recently acquired a tractor and was very proudly driving it everywhere, so that everybody should know he'd got it. All tractors supplied at this time had iron spade lugs instead of rubber tyres on the wheels, but bands were supplied for road use. Amos Bloxham was quick to notice the absence of these bands and immediately tried to show his authority as local road man. "Hey there, you've no business driving that tractor on the road, Len Wilson, you'm damaging the surface of the road. I shall have to report thee to the Council."

"Get your hair cut, Amos!" retorted Wilson.

"Ah you can gyule, Len Wilson, I've seen 'ee up to yer tricks with

147

them wenches, I've seen 'ee, and don't say I ain't, 'cos I 'ave. I'll report 'ee for that as well while I'm about it, you see if I don't."

"You always was a nasty mischief making old varmint, Amos. If you don't shut your gob I'll lay into you," retorted Len Wilson.

"Ooh, ooh, just listen to that," said one of the women.

"Yes," said another, "I've not got much time for Amos, but it's time somebody did something about that dirty old Len Wilson."

"Ah, but it don't do to say anything," said a third woman.

"Len Wilson's too free with his hands," said Mrs. Elford.

"My Fred would give him what for, if he touched me," said Mrs. Jenkins.

"So degrading," said Mrs. Peabody.

*　*　*　*

The bearded man jumped about and tore at his hair, imploring Fred to do something to stop those wretched women's prattle. Eventually, the bearded man got his silence and was able to start recording. He made some introductory remarks and then handed the microphone over to a small woman wearing a scarlet coat and purple stockings — purple stockings, something that none of us had ever seen before, and all of the onlookers were rather shocked.

"Oooh, naughty colours!" came from a woman in the crowd.

"I'll bet she's a fast hussy," said Mrs..Gerrish.

Len Wilson gave Purple Stockings an appraising look and Amos Bloxham could be heard muttering, "Look at that, a cockin' 'er arse."

Purple Stockings took the microphone, and, as she stepped delicately over half a dozen small Christmas trees, she said, "Here I am, climbing over thousands and thousands of Christmas Trees."

"Knees up, Mother Brown" came from someone in the crowd.

The bearded man waved his arm and waggled his head and Charlie, one of his staff, was sent to silence the interrupter. Charlie smelt of perfume, and was wearing a top coat of pale grey with an astrakhan collar.

Purple Stockings continued with the recording quite unperturbed and after a while she said, "And now I'm going to interview some of the men who ensure that you still get a Christmas tree..." The Stationmaster adjusted his braided cap, twirled the ends of his moustache, beamed and stepped forward, but she ignored him and thrust the microphone under the nose of Owen Tishworth. Somebody in the crowd laughed at the Stationmaster's obvious discomfort and said, "Not you, General, sit down." There was a ripple of laughter and the bearded man flung his arms in the air.

The startled Owen jumped back a yard from the microphone, but Purple Stockings caught hold of his arm and said to him, "You are the man who brings the trees to the station from the plantation, tell us about the plantation and how the trees are grown."

Owen agreed that it was he who brought the trees to the station and with much humming and hawing and er-ering, he described the cultivation of the trees. The Stationmaster then spoke, reading from a scrap of paper held in his left hand, his right hand kept busy tugging at his moustache. Without waiting for an invitation Uncle George lumbered forward. "Good awfternoon," he said, "fust I'll say a few words about gardening and then if I've time I'll allude briefly to pigs."

There was a round of applause from the crowd and cries of "Good old George!" Reuben shouted, "That's the style, George, keep at it ole fella, you tell 'em." I felt a lump come in my throat, tears came to my eyes and my heart swelled with pride. Uncle George waved a nonchalant hand and gave a broad wink in acknowledgement. His voice became louder, "It's high time you had your winter broad beans in."

The bearded man signalled frantically to Purple Stockings, but Uncle George now had the microphone grasped in both of his large horny hands. "If you ain't got 'em in yet, for goodness sake hurry up, broad beans are first class grub. And next year try to get 'em in earlier. Get the dung on to your garden now and dig it in, that artificial manure's no bottle." Uncle was shouting now and waving the microphone in his enthusiasm. "Get some big flower pots, old buckets or cider barrels and straw ready for forcing your rhubarb, rhubarb is wonderful stuff for opening the bowels. The curse of the country's constipation, the bowels must be opened, and there's nothing like fresh green vegetables for opening 'em. Grunting and heavin' and strainin' on the privy is no good to you, if you take my advice and grow plenty ... hey, hey, stand back there, my man, I'm broadcasting now."

Charlie was pushing and pulling at Uncle. "Now, where was I afore that varmint started his fiddle faddling? — oh ah, I know, if you listen carefully to me you'll be able to grow some master vegetables — get out of the way, you nogman." Uncle George hit out with a spatulate hand and sent Charlie reeling backwards.

"Go on, George, me old beauty, that'll quamp'm," shouted Reuben.

The bearded man and Fred closed in on Uncle George, Charlie approached cautiously. "Make your plans for next year now, get your seed lists ..." There was a scuffle round the microphone, Uncle George red in the face cried, "Now you've got me moithered with yer slack, shut thee rattle oot!" The bearded man was hissing to Charlie, "Get that old fool out of the way." Uncle George heard him and gave him a hard look, saying, "None of your insubordination, young fella m'lad." Then Uncle pursed his lips and blew out his cheeks and stared even harder at the bearded man in dark glasses before bellowing, "Rajah rhubarb! It's my opinion that you're a confounded spy!"

"Stop the recording!" yelled the bearded man and snatched the microphone from Uncle George's hand. Fred and Charlie grabbed Uncle by both arms and pushed him roughly aside.

"'Pon my soul," said a bewildered Uncle George, "this is a terrible way of goin' on, and I ain't hardly started the gardening talk."

The crowd was dumbfounded. I looked round for Mother and noticed she had the saucer eyes and disapproving look. Mrs. Peabody and Mrs. Gosworth were tight lipped. Aunt Aggie broke the silence, "If this is broadcasting, I don't want my Sam to take it up, the poor old fellow'd never stand it."

Uncle George, after a few vigorous protests, ambled away towards the porters' room. Soon after, people lost interest in the broadcast, which in any case was in complete disarray. The crowd slowly dispersed; I waited for Uncle to come out of the porters' room.

Uncle George and I walked home from the station together. We both felt upset about the whole broadcasting business. Uncle George said to me, "The damned nogmen, they didn't give me a chance to get into my stride, but never mind, boy, there's always another day." I bit my lip and nodded my head in agreement. "But, rajah rhubarb!" rumbled Uncle George. "They can't keep a good man down."

ENDS